THE PRIVATE MONEY GUIDE

SOLUTIONS TO FINDING MONEY: WHERE TO GO AND HOW TO ASK

REAL ESTATE EDITION
BY CHRIS NAUGLE

Copyright ©2018 by Chris Naugle

All rights reserved.

Disclaimer & FTC Notice

No part of this book may be reproduced or transmitted in any form, by anyone or by any means, electronic, mechanical, or digital including photocopying or recording, or by the information storage and retrieval system, without written permission by the author.

While attempts have been made to verify the information provided in this publication, neither the author nor the publisher assumes any responsibility for errors, omissions, or contrary interpretations of the subject matter herein.

This book is for entertainment purposes only. The views expressed are those of the author alone and should not be taken as expert instructions or commands. The reader is responsible for his or her own actions.

Adherence to all applicable laws and regulations, including international, federal, state, provincial, and local governing professional licensing, business practices, advertising, and all other aspects of doing business in the US, Canada or any other jurisdiction is the sole responsibility of the purchaser or reader.

Neither the author nor the publisher assumes any responsibility or liability whatsoever on the behalf of the purchaser or reader of these materials.

Any perceived slight of any individual or organization is purely of these materials.

I sometimes use affiliate links in the content. This means if you decide to make a purchase, I will get a small sales commission. I only endorse products that I have personally used or trust and have found useful. Please make sure and do your own research before making any purchase online.

All translations of this document must be approved in writing by the author. You can contact Flipout Academy for permission to translate or reproduce this and for distribution agreements. Printed in the United States of America.

To order copies for you or your business, go to www.chrisnaugle.com.

You can also email contact@chrisnaugle.com or

call Flipout Academy at (716) 800-1892.

Written By: Chris Naugle

Edited By: Lorissa Naugle

Illustrated By: Shawna Decker

First Edition 1.1

A Free Gift to Help You Get A Fast Start

I am honored that you chose to pick up my book. I know your time is valuable and choosing to spend that time reading this book means a lot to me personally. I hope you will gain from my material, my story and my experiences, to get out of this book what you are looking for. I have followed many successful people in an effort to learn the secrets of their success and it always points back to one concept. In its simplest form successful people get very good at two things; investing their time and their money to further their success. I would like to repay that favor in a small way with a little bonus for those who buy the book!

To be successful in real estate you must become good at many things. I feel the two most important things are:

1) Finding lucrative deals at the right price

2) Finding the money to buy these properties

In an effort to simplify how to do these two things very well I have created guides that provide you the necessary information you will need to do these two things better. I wanted to provide you with these two guides as a free gift.

To get access to these bonus guides just follow the instructions below.

Text "Flipout" to 314-665-1767

Contents

Preface 1
Chapter 1 ....
   Biggest Barrier of Entry Into Real Estate Investing 7
Chapter 2 ....
   Money Sources 11
Chapter 3 ....
   Finding the Deal 41
Chapter 4 ....
   Analysis & Strategy 45
Chapter 5 ....
   Structuring the Deal 51
Chapter 6 ....
   The Perfect Loan Proposal 63
Chapter 7 ....
   Execution 79
Chapter 8 ....
   Second Phase of Financing 87
Chapter 9 ....
   Get to Your Goal Faster 91
Chapter 10 ....
   Strategies to Cashing Out 95

Preface

It is so important for you to know that I was raised in a lower middle-class family and no one in my extended family was wealthy or even came close. I had such big dreams and lots of ambition growing up but my desires came to a halt when they required money. As a teenager, I worked at a small farm in the mornings and a restaurant in the evenings. The manager of the restaurant degraded me so badly during my shifts that I left work constantly feeling like I was hopeless and worthless. After weeks of entering work with a knot in the pit of my stomach, it got to the point where I couldn't take the unwarranted verbal abuse any longer and one night after he had name-called me, I plucked up enough courage to get in his face and scream, "I QUIT!"

This was the critical moment that defined the rest of my life; it happened when I was only 16 years old. Younger than most in making this decision, I made a promise to myself that I would never work for anyone else ever again. But, I knew I still needed to make money for my car expenses and wanted spending money for travelling to snowboard events. Unlike my friends, I didn't have the leisure of asking my mom for 20 bucks whenever I wanted.

After tossing a few ideas around in my mind, I decided to start a clothing line out of my basement. I knew there was an opportunity to make money at it because I could sell the line at the skateboard and snowboard competitions I entered. I'll never forget coming home after work that night to tell my mom about my grandiose idea. I not only had her support, but she also became one of my seamstresses. I called the new apparel line, Phat Clothing Company, and it blended my love for snowboarding and my need for income harmoniously. I was able to start Phat Clothing Company with a $500 loan from the bank and it was backed by a dream. That small clothing line would soon turn into a Western New York chain of skateboard & snowboard stores called Phatman Board Shops.

Many years later, after the recession in the early 2000's, I was forced to get a second job that landed me in the financial services Industry. What started as a temporary part-time job turned out to be something I loved. In my first year I had made $76,000 which was more money than I had made in all of the years I owned the board shops. I consolidated my retail stores down to two locations and in 2006 I franchised Phatman and sold one of those two stores. This enabled me to focus more time on my financial advisory business which was doing very well. I remained a licensed financial advisor with many other accreditations until I sold my book of business in 2018.

In 2006 I started my first flip.

In 2007 I finished that first flip.

In 2008 I decided to purchase a dilapidated retail strip mall that would be my first commercial development project and the future home of Phatman. This was a crazy idea and I had to borrow over $300,000 from a group of hard money lenders to make it happen. This was my first experience with hard money lenders and it proved to be a hard lesson. Halfway through renovations, the 2008 market downturn started and I was quickly running out of money to pay these lenders the insane interest payments that I had agreed upon. As things worsened with the economy, my financial advisory business came to almost a dead halt and Phatman's profits dropped 30% overnight! I was about two months away from going bankrupt.

I'm not the type of person to believe in luck, but what happened next was as close to luck as I've ever seen. I managed to rent the other three units in the plaza and because the plaza was then occupied, I was able to get a local community bank to refinance the deal so I could pay those hard money lenders back. I thanked God for this because these lenders were the type of people who not only would have foreclosed on my property, but also would have taken off a few of my fingers had I defaulted on the loan.

In 2009 I was back at it, buying rundown apartment buildings for pennies on the dollar. By 2014 I had built up a rental portfolio of 36 units. This would seem like a dream come true but, in reality, I was so broke that I had to ask Lorissa, my girlfriend at the time (now wife) to help me pay the utility bills and my mortgage. I sold Phatman in 2010 to free up time and to help fund this real estate venture.

Lorissa and I even sold our big, beautiful house that we treasured because we still needed more money to keep the machine going.

We had to make very difficult decisions, which included living in one of our apartments and living extremely frugal to get where we are today. We had to tell our friends, "No, sorry, we can't attend" way too often. At the time, we thought that the struggle would never end… but now looking back, it was only for a fraction of time. On a positive note, we never had to claim bankruptcy and the sacrifices we made ensured to us that we could get through anything.

Let's look at where I was financially, in more depth. I had 36 rented units and I was worth quite a bit on paper so how could I be broke? The answer is simple, I did not understand how money worked in real estate. You see, I used banks to fund each deal. That means they gave me 80% of the purchase price, and I had used my own money to do the renovations and to pay the remaining 20% plus closing costs. Every time I would get a little money, I would dive back into another deal which would send me deeper and deeper into debt. In 2014 I sold every property I owned, and to my surprise, it was very profitable! This is when it came to me that I didn't know what I didn't know. There had to be an easier way to get these deals funded. I needed to learn about money. I needed to gain more knowledge. I needed to be educated on how the real estate business actually worked. This is where it all changed. We went ahead and spent over $80,000 being educated and mentored by some of the best real estate investors in the business. We racked up our credit cards for our education because we didn't *have* the money in full, but we *could* make payments. We knew we couldn't turn back once we were committed. Once those cards were swiped, it was go time. Today, my wife and I own seven companies, we founded Flipout Academy which is a results-based education system that focuses on our students' success, we had our own TV show "Risky Builders" air on HGTV along with a couple of our flips featured on two other HGTV shows, we hold over $8,000,000 in real estate, we have done well over 200 deals since 2014 and we live the life we used to dream about. The greatest part is that the best is yet to come! I can tell you this: the same can be true for you. But first, you must understand this: <u>money has always been and will always be the most important tool</u> you will ever use to build the life you want.

Let me tell you what I wish I had learned when I started...

Like I mentioned earlier, my first real estate deal was a flip in 2006 at the age of 28. I was doing well as a financial advisor and owned two profitable retail stores, but I was not in a good financial position by any means, as I was simply getting by. It wasn't long before a realtor showed me a deal that looked like a great flip. Based on my (in hindsight, flawed) calculations, I thought I could make $35,000 on this one deal. At that point in my life, this sort of money was a game changer. This deal looked like it was the answer to so many of my problems. The first step was to find financing for this deal. This proved to be challenging because I had no idea where to look for money to invest in real estate. I decided to take the most logical route at the time and ask a bank for the money. This is where I began to realize how difficult this process could be. After a month of back-and-forth with necessary documents and an endless list of tasks, I received a commitment letter for far less than I needed. I was under the impression that the bank would give me the money I needed for rehab plus the purchase price but, I quickly learned that was *not* going to be the case. They would only lend 80% of purchase price and not a penny of the costs I would incur from renovating the property. Now I had a dilemma; I had to find the remaining money in only one week. The next idea that came into my head was to ask everyone I knew for a loan. After hearing the word, "no" way too many times to count, I decided to max out my credit cards and take the maximum amount in loans from my life insurance policies, which ended up being *just* enough to revamp the property. After I was finished with renovations, I decided to rent it out for a year then sell it for a profit. The downside is that the profit was only $8,000, nowhere near the $35,000 I was originally expecting. Even though it was not even close to my projected profit, it was enough to get me hooked on real estate and I became extremely motivated to learn how this industry worked in the capacity of flipping houses, creating passive income, and ultimately becoming the bank.

When executed properly, real estate has the ability to allow you to further your goals and to help you live the life you've always dreamed of. This is my give back to you so that you can avoid making the same mistakes I did when I first started out. Please know that I can't elaborate on every single one-off situation since all deals are structured differently. However, you'll soon understand the process of money in real estate and this will guide you through the secrets of money and how to implement what I do within your own deals. This is not a *get rich quick scheme* or even a simple answer to all of real estate related problems. I started with close to nothing and we have built an empire. No matter what your circumstances are, no matter where you are in life, this process will work. However, it will not be easy and it will take time. I believe it is your responsibility to chase your dreams and never let anyone tell you that you can't do the things you want to do or have the things that you want to have. I give you permission to dream the craziest dreams, and one day watch those dreams unfold because of your hard work. No matter how old you are, don't let the fear of money stop you. Remember, **money** is just a tool.

Chapter 1
Biggest Barrier of Entry into Real Estate Investing

Money is the one thing that most people have all wrong in real estate. We all use it as an excuse; a crutch. We tend to think and say, "I would love to do real estate but, I don't have enough money." Or my favorite excuse is... "when this or that happens, I will invest in real estate." The fact of the matter is, in real estate, and in life, <u>it is never about your actual resources, it is about how resourceful you can be!</u>

Fear is what drives this reaction to be negative, to make excuses, to think and to talk yourself out of your dreams. The right thing to do is start right here and right now. No more excuses! If money is something that has held you back then you will find this information fascinating and incredibly useful.

Let's start with some facts of why real estate is so unique and how <u>money is all around you</u> just waiting for you to ask for it.

Real estate is a <u>tangible asset</u>: That asset can be <u>leveraged</u>, that asset can be <u>insured</u>, that asset can be <u>improved to force appreciation</u>, that asset can <u>provide passive income</u> through rents, and that asset will always <u>be in demand</u> no matter what happens.

Real Estate can <u>secure and protect an investment</u>. First, you must learn how to <u>buy real estate for the right price</u>. Once you have that figured out, you have figured out the hardest part.

Once you learn how to find the deals, you can make money so many ways —even if you never buy the property. We cover that strategy in my other book, *'The Raw and Uncensored Guide to Wholesaling.'*

Did you know that <u>real property will never be worth nothing?</u>

Unlike other investments such as stocks, bonds, mutual funds, and many others that are available and recommended, <u>real estate is an asset that can go up and down in value but, it cannot go to $0</u>. Some of you are thinking, well if it burns down or if a natural disaster destroys the property it can. My answer to that is, I sure hope you were smart enough to buy insurance! You must understand the significance of insurance— specifically full replacement value policies, and they will be mandatory with each application in dealing with the money sources you will learn about. You have to <u>protect your investors and your investment</u> and that is where a good insurance policy is essential. There are investor-friendly insurance brokers who can assist you with coverage.

Let me tell you a story. In 2008 while I was deep into my plaza development, we had a freak snow storm here in Buffalo, New York that resulted in over three feet of snow in less than 36 hours. It's pretty common for the snow to fall rapidly here in Buffalo, but what followed next is not common. That three feet of snow all melted in less than 24 hours! This caused massive flooding. My strip mall completely flooded in the process! I had tens of thousands of dollars in materials, tools and supplies that in an instant, were destroyed. My first reaction was to panic. I was already behind schedule, over budget and running out of money to pay these hard money lenders back, and now I lost everything I needed to finish in the blink of an eye. Luckily, I had this property insured and after a few days, I was handed a check for the full value of all the losses, the cleanup, and the remediation. Had I forgot that one critical step, I would have been bankrupt, and I certainly would have lost the property and maybe a few fingers.

The reason so many of us allow money to be our crutch has so much to do with living in a judgmental society and dealing with people who have a 'know-it-all' mentality and fearful mindsets. In our lives, we have naysayers telling us we can't do this or we can't do that, or they give us their opinion on our ideas without ever actually trying (said idea) themselves.

They always know someone who tried getting into what we want to, but failed miserably, and they tell us those stories to try to protect us. They provide us with advice about the direction of our life. Unfortunately, these people are often the ones closest to us: family members and friends. We all have had someone stand in the way of our dreams. You have to make a decision to delicately (or not so delicately) tell them that this is ultimately your decision, your goal, and your dream. You must ask them to support you. If they can't, then say goodbye temporarily. This will not be easy, but you do not need someone standing in the way and telling you, "I told you so," every single time something goes wrong. <u>You MUST surround yourself with like-minded people</u>. People who have succeeded and who are successful. People doing exactly what you want to be doing. Your journey will be full of negative people I like to call them "dream killers." I can tell you from personal experience and from other stories I've heard from successful people, that the ones who are trying to give you advice and protect you will later be your biggest supporters. However, not until you are successful… so move those people out and begin your new venture without them.

Chapter 2
Money Sources

8 Resources You Can Tap Into

Money is all around us. It is plentiful and there is no shortage of it at all. You need to learn where all this money is, how to find it and how to ask the right questions in order to obtain it.

Most of us have checking and savings accounts. These accounts are used to pay bills, fund occasional vacations, and provide needed resources if things don't go as planned. Although most people have money in checking and savings accounts, this will be one of the last places we look for money. The reason is because people view this money as being untouchable, or sacred, and they certainly aren't going to risk losing their emergency money. In their minds it's their only money, and they don't spend it other than for living and saving, and the occasional gift giving. <u>The money we need to look for is money that people view as long term money,</u> or phantom money.

Everything we will talk about in this booklet revolves around building relationships. The relationships you will build with lenders will be critical to your success. Lenders can be anyone from a personal friend to an established private lending company and therefore we refer to them as relationship-based lenders. There are technically three distinctive types of private lenders. Each of the three types are based on the relationship between the borrower and the lender.

The three types of lenders can be categorized as follows:

- Primary Circle: Family & Close Friends
- Secondary Circle: Colleagues, Friends of Friends, Personal and Professional Acquaintances

- Third-Party Circle: Accredited Investors and Hard Money Lenders

The next two resources we are going to discuss will be better suited for your Primary Circle and possibly your Secondary Circle. They will require you to have established relationships and trust.

Resource #1
Hidden Equity

Over the last few years one thing is certain: real estate values have been steadily increasing. There are some areas across the country that have seen a tremendous amount of growth. This means that almost anyone who has a primary residence, which they have owned for 5-10 years or longer (but haven't refinanced in a few years) has hidden equity available. Any smart financial guru will tell you that having equity is great, but if that money is not put into motion, it's a waste. Money must be sent to work just like you have to go to work. The thing people don't understand is equity in your home will never change your situation unless that equity is tapped into and put to work to make more money. Your job is to tell people how to do this. Since most homeowners likely have equity, you need to know how to get this money. The easiest way to do this is through a HELOC (Home Equity Line of Credit). Most banks will gladly open a HELOC with very little effort, low costs, and only a little bit of paperwork. In my experience it takes less than 30 days to tap this resource. Banks understand equity and the safety of real estate security, therefore they are more willing to lend you money using HELOCs.

The process is pretty simple to get a HELOC. First, the bank will require some basic paperwork including an application, tax returns, and a credit report. If they find your financial situation to be acceptable, they will issue you the line of credit and you will be able to use your home's equity. The interest rates on HELOCs are typically low since these loans are secured by real estate.

But what happens if you can't access equity either because your credit score is too low, you haven't owned your home long enough to get a HELOC or you don't own a home at all? No worries, you still have options. Just about everyone knows at least one person who has owned their own home for long enough to have built up enough equity for you to use. Now all you have to do is structure a win-win situation. First you must have a subject property either identified or even better, under contract. Next, you will show them how they are going to make money in your deal. Here is an example:

$100,000   Loan

x 5%   HELOC Interest Rate

= $5,000/year, $416.67/month interest-only payment

If you went to this person and asked for a $100,000 loan and offered 10% interest, here's what the numbers would look like:

$100,000   private loan for your deal

x 10%   simple interest

=$10,000/year, $833.33/month

To sum it up, the lender would net $5,000 in interest payments after paying the interest payment on the HELOC.

I don't know about you, but I sure wouldn't mind an extra $5,000 per year for doing nothing more than tapping equity. You can loan your money or you can borrow other people's money. I hope now you can see how simple and lucrative this sort of deal can be. Later in this booklet, we will cover how to structure this deal so that all parties are protected. For right now, I simply want you to change your mindset and think about where you can find money.

Resource #2
401K and Employer-Sponsored Retirement Accounts

You probably have been told a hundred times that it is important to save for your retirement and that you should put away 5-20% from each paycheck. For some of you, retirement is a really long time away, but nevertheless, it *is* important, and you're never too young to plan for your financial future.

A 401(k) plan is a tax-qualified, defined-contribution pension account. Your retirement savings contributions are sometimes matched by your employer, which is free money to you. These funds are deducted from your paycheck before taxation (these contributions are tax-deferred until withdrawn after retirement or as otherwise permitted by applicable law). The amounts are limited to a maximum pre-tax annual contribution of $18,500 (as of 2018). Some of you might have other employer-provided defined-contribution plans such as 403(b) plans for non-profit institutions, or 457(b) plans for governmental employers.

The reason I bring up retirement accounts is that these types of accounts represent literally tens of trillions of dollars you could use to fund your real estate investments. Most people view retirement savings as long-term money, that is, money they cannot use until someday later in life (59 1/2 is the actual age you can access these accounts without penalty). If this money cannot be accessed, then why are we discussing it? Because most people don't realize they can make money using these accounts. In my experience, this is money most investors ARE willing to discuss if you explain to them how it works. Some people will think that they can't use their 401(k) or retirement account because it will be taxed and penalized. Luckily for you, there's a way to use the money in a retirement account that won't incur any taxes or penalties. Most plans will allow the owner to take a loan from their retirement account. (Not all plans allow this though so it's important to have the owner check with the HR department or the plan administrator before pursuing this option). If it's allowed, most plans limit the amount you can borrow to $50,000 or 50% of the value of the 401k—whichever is less. Most plans also require you to repay the loan in full within five years.

Now that you are aware that money can be taken as a loan without being taxed and penalized, we have just identified a massive resource to tap into. Taking a loan against a retirement account isn't like getting "free" money—or is it? The owner will have to pay interest on the loan, and usually your plan administrator will add 1-2 percentage points above the prime rate. The good news is that the interest payments go back into the retirement account, so the interest is being paid back to the owner. If it's your account, then it's being paid back to you! It's important to remember that if you take out a loan against your 401k, the loan *must* be repaid by the deadline. Otherwise, the loan is considered to be an early withdrawal and you will be assessed taxes and penalties on the loan. Remember, if you lose your job in the interim, or are unable to pay, it could cost a lot more than what you had anticipated. Also, I do have to disclose that there's no guarantee that your real estate investment will generate a higher return than stocks, mutual funds, and exchange-traded funds (called ETFs) that your retirement plan is already invested in. The stock market has been on a tear lately, generating high double-digit returns over the past year but the bull market certainly won't last forever. The stock market is cyclical; sometimes it's high, sometimes it's low. Right now, my opinion is that we are at the end of the bull market and the markets will correct or move to a bearish cycle in the near future. Warren Buffett said it best, "it is wise to be fearful when others are greedy, and greedy when others are fearful." Most retirement accounts have had significant gains over the past few years.

I can show you how to take profits off the table and make a fixed interest rate on your retirement account.

Here's how it works: you take a loan from your 401(k), which means you have up to 5 years to repay the loan. Let's assume for this example that the interest rate you will be charged on the loan is 5% (remember, this interest is paid back to your retirement account) then, you invest the money you get from the loan into a real estate deal. Most hard money or private money loans charge interest rates of 7-15% with astronomical fees, so if you offered to pay 10% to the lender for taking a loan from their 401(k), you would be able to save a lot in fees and interest while giving them a piece of the pie in the form of a higher interest rate than they could earn elsewhere.

If you went to the owner of the retirement account and asked for a $100,000 loan but offered to give them 10% interest, here's what the numbers would look like:

$100,000 private loan for your deal

x 5% interest charged on the loan from the retirement account

= $5,000/year, $416.67/month

$100,000 private loan for your deal

x 10% simple interest

= $10,000/year, $833.33/month

This means the owner of the retirement account earns $5,000 per year / $416.67 per month (plus, the interest they pay on the 401(k) loan goes back in their retirement account.

If you can explain to people how they can take a loan from their 401(k) account and make an extra 5% *fixed* on top of what they are paying back to themselves secured by a first position lien on the piece of real estate, now you have their undivided attention.

When I was still working as a financial advisor, I had a 401(k) that I contributed 15% of my paycheck into. In the beginning of my real estate journey, I would use my 401(k) loans to buy rentals. This added to the already decent returns that I was making on my real estate deals. Who wouldn't want an extra 5% on all their deals?

Chapter 2: Money Sources

You too, can lend your money out to other people and make 10-15% with no work involved at all. This was an eye-opener for me and this is exactly how I need you to start thinking. Think like the bank and teach others how to think like the bank.

The easiest money in real estate is made when you are asleep. This can be accomplished a few ways, through rental portfolios or by becoming the bank and loaning your funds to other people for their real estate deals. Let them do the work. <u>You provide the money and you secure your money with the real estate deal.</u>

This is how you tap into the resources that most people are not thinking about. You must show people how this works and how lucrative it can be for them. This strategy works best in down markets or when the stock market is at a high point, and fear is setting in, and the media starts talking about the end of a bull-market. This is happening right now and I am seeing new signs every day. No one likes losing money on their investments. However, no one knows when the stock market is going to go down either.

Resource #3
Mutual Funds, Stocks, Non-Qualified Investment Accounts and Certificates of Deposit

These resources are similar to what I mentioned earlier when discussing checking and savings accounts. These sources are not as sacred, but they will present some interesting challenges when you try to tap into them. The type of accounts I am referring to are any investment account that is not a retirement account. These accounts are typically very accessible. When people have strong profits and the markets are doing very well, it is wise to take some or all profits off the table to shield against future losses. As Warren Buffet says, "buy low, sell high" … and I add, "don't lose money." This is something people are talking about and they are looking for ways to invest that are not correlated to the stock market. You hold the answer to what many investors are seeking: high, fixed-rate of returns and asset-backed collateral. In my experience, this resource has been extremely useful for fast closes, transition funding, or extremely short-term deals like a wholesale deal or a paint and carpet fix and flip that can be sold quickly. I have also tapped into this resource for rehab funds in a second lien secured position (deals where I use bank funding to buy the house and then use money from one of these funds to pay for my rehab costs). It is important to remember that if you use private investor funds and they are in a second position, be sure that the property has adequate equity to support the debt. I typically make sure each deal never exceeds 70-80% of ARV (After Repair Value). By maintaining 70-80%, you are always certain that, if needed, you can seek bank funding that will be sufficient enough to cover the loans on the property. I always plan for an exit on every deal I do. This way, I never get into a situation where I need to liquidate assets to cover the loans. The main thing to remember when tapping this source of funding is that people will be seeking an interest rate higher than what they have been getting on their current investments. In a strong bull market this may be a tough conversation. In a bear market when the stock market is down, this will be a much easier conversation to have. Lastly, I mentioned Certificates of Deposit as a potential source. CDs typically pay low interest rates and are FDIC insured. Most investors that buy CDs do so because they are seeking guarantees which you cannot offer. <u>*Never* guarantee returns or interest rates in any situation. You cannot provide guarantees under any situation and it's illegal to do so.</u>

Resource #4
The Trillion-Dollar Source

This is the most important thing I can teach you.

This section will talk about a massive resource called IRAs, old retirement accounts, and self-directed IRAs. Individual retirement accounts are one of the largest pools of money out there. How large? Well...over 2 trillion dollars in the United States alone! I mentioned this when discussing the 401(k) strategy but it should be mentioned again. The stock market has been doing really well the past few years, which means it may be time to think about taking profits and gains off the table. Here are a few reasons why I feel it is time to rethink your strategy for your IRA accounts.

One of the hardest things for most investors and their advisors to do is decide when the right time is to start selling off either all, or some of their investment portfolio. We get stuck in a pattern, a pattern of thinking that the market and the investments will keep going up. For me, the time has arrived to take profits off the table on *almost* all of my stock market investments. Now don't get me wrong, I am *not* selling my entire portfolio and moving to cash. It is simply time to reposition my investments into alternative investments that are not correlated to the stock market. The market is simply starting to look a bit dangerous. I'm also seeing patterns develop that scare me to death and I am convinced a correction is coming in the near future.

The Federal Reserve has kept interest rates at an all-time low for far too long. Stocks have an inverse relationship to bonds. When interest rates go up, bond prices go down. If rates go up too fast it drives bond prices lower, which eventually has a breaking point. You see, if the proverbial bubble were to burst in the bond market, interest rates could skyrocket in a short period of time. This has happened in the past. Do you remember when the former Fed chair, Janet Yellen, told the world that her desire was to start straightening out the Fed's 4.5 trillion dollar balance sheet? This was not a bad thing, but straightening this out at a time when interest rates are rising is risky. It is all about <u>liquidity in the system</u>. The central bank withdraws liquidity by selling its bond holdings. In turn, this will drive long-term interest rates higher. As I mentioned earlier, bond prices move inversely to interest rates, therefore, bond prices could plummet.

Ever since the stock market hit its lowest point in 2009, all three major indices, the DOW Jones, S&P 500 and the NASDAQ have returned triple digits or higher. One reason for these huge market moves during President Obama's term was all the money and liquidity the Fed pumped into the system. This was one of the main reasons why the markets and our economy did not collapse. The Obama stimulus and the liquidity the government pumped into the economy by buying bonds is what saved the markets. If they hadn't done so, the liquidity would have dried up and more banks would have failed.

Another thing to consider: what happens when corporate earnings decline from today's speculative expectation? In my opinion, I feel this is currently keeping stock prices artificially high. I believe this is happening now and it has been happening for a few years already.

Any way you look at it, stock prices can't remain at these levels. The markets have always gone up and down in very predictable patterns. These patterns and market cycles should not be ignored. The last thing to pay very close attention to is M&A activity. M&A means mergers and acquisitions, which, if you haven't noticed, have been happening at extremely high levels. Companies are gobbling up competitors and other companies to gain market share and increase earnings to help their earnings grow for greedy stockholders. When companies cannot grow organically, they turn to mergers and acquisitions. However, buying up other companies when the markets and the economy are at high levels means paying a premium price for the purchase. Not only is paying too much for something concerning to me, it almost always results in speculation of future expectations. Which is even more dangerous. This is exactly what has been happening lately and its happening at extremely dangerous levels.

Now that I have completely bored you with my old financial advisory opinions, let's discuss what real estate can do for returns; especially for retirement account returns.

<u>Real estate can provide a great alternative to stocks</u>, so let's get into how this works.

Now before we begin, I want to be completely transparent on a few things and I need you to understand what a self-directed IRA/SDIRA is:

A self-directed individual retirement account (SDIRA) is an individual retirement account (IRA) in which the investor is in charge of making all the investment decisions. The term "self-directed IRA" is bit of a misnomer because all IRAs are self-directed; you decide where to invest your IRA funds. The self-directed IRA provides the investor with greater opportunity for asset diversification outside of the traditional stocks, bonds, and mutual funds. Self-directed IRAs can invest in real estate, private market securities and more. All securities and investments are held in an account administered by a custodian or trustee.

Now that you understand what a SDIRA is, here are some pitfalls to using them that you must be familiar with:

First, self-directed IRAs have a lot of rules and these rules are very important to understand to and abide by.

Here is a link to a FAQ that should give you an idea of these rules: https://www.horizontrust.com/learn-the-4-step-process-of-self-directed-iras/frequently-asked-questions-about-self-directing/

Secondly, what I am going to explain does not involve you using your SDIRA to buy real estate. You can do this, but I do not recommend it. There are so many ways to make a mistake and one mistake could cost you a lot of money in taxes and penalties. I am only referring to using SDIRAs to loan money to others for secured real estate deals.

A self-directed IRA is a type of traditional or Roth IRA that is used to save for retirement and is structured in such a way that it facilitates withdrawals at a specified age. Self-directed IRAs are different from traditional IRAs and Roth IRAs only by the assets they hold. These accounts are designed for DIY (do-it-yourself) investors and allow their owner to invest in a much broader array of securities than with a traditional or Roth IRA. Because these accounts are administered by their owner, they require greater involvement and due diligence by you.

Investors seeking a SDIRA will have to look for a brokerage that specializes in these types of accounts. These companies are willing to serve as the custodian for the SDIRA investment assets. Some SDIRA companies still impose constraints on the holdings of the fund, so it is important to ensure that the account allows you to invest your funds in a way that makes sense based on your overall financial plan. Some SDIRAs may specialize in specific alternative assets such as private equity or private debt.

It is the responsibility of the investor to comply with all Internal Revenue Service (IRS) regulations for IRAs. Because a SDIRA allows for such a broad portfolio, its holdings have greater risk of breaching IRS regulations and therefore require greater caution from investors, specifically when investing in real estate. SDIRAs have the same eligibility and contribution rules applied to all IRAs. Where <u>SDIRA investors must be cautious is in the personal use of assets held in the portfolio.</u> <u>The IRS does not allow IRA investments to be used for any personal use until the targeted withdrawal date.</u> This can specifically pertain to real estate held in a portfolio and does not allow the investor to invest in real estate for personal use. The IRS also requires that IRA assets are held by a <u>qualified SDIRA trustee or custodian.</u>

As is the case with traditional or Roth IRAs, SDIRAs can include nearly any type of investment. They can accommodate private securities, real estate, limited partnerships, precious metals, commodities, crowdfunding investments and more. But life insurance is not permitted in an SDIRA.

You will not see self-directed IRAs advertised alongside traditional and Roth IRAs at mainstream brokerage firms. Investors seeking a self-directed IRA will typically need to open an account with a specialized firm that offers qualified SDIRA custody services. These firms will hold assets in an SDIRA for the plan owner and help to monitor how those funds are used to ensure it complies with IRS tax regulations. SDIRA custodians leave the investment decisions to the SDIRA owner and allow the investor to build a comprehensive portfolio that includes nearly any type of investment.

Self-directed.org provides a comprehensive list of SDIRA custodians available for investors. Since the range of services that are offered can vary from one SDIRA custodian to another, fees typically vary as well. SDIRAs usually require an annual custodian fee. SDIRA custodians are willing to provide a range of customized services for a fee. Some examples of fees charged by SDIRAs include one-time establishment fee, first-year annual fee, annual renewal fee, and fees for investment bill paying.

Read more: *Self-Directed IRA - (SDIRA)* *https://www.investopedia.com/terms/s/self-directed-ira.asp#ixzz5Ufa9Y8Pr*

Source: Investopedia

Now you have an understanding of what an SDIRA is and how they operate, so let's talk about how you can use SDIRAs to find money for your real estate deals. It is relatively simple; all you need to do is be the expert in explaining how people with old 401(k)s and IRAs can diversify by lending money from their SDIRA. These people are called private investors and they will be explained in greater detail later on in this booklet. In this section, I want to explain the strategy in such a way that you will be able to explain it to potential investors.

When explaining how to use a SDIRA to fund a deal break down the process into the following six steps:

Step 1: Open a self-directed retirement account with a qualified custodian.

Most of us are used to the big brokerage houses acting as the custodian for our retirement savings accounts. However, those firms only permit investors to invest in publicly traded securities and just for the record, a personal loan is not an option here. There are many companies that specialize in helping you self-direct your investments as well as other alternative investments.

Step 2: Have an attorney write and review the note for the hard money loan.

Thoroughly review the note to be sure it is agreeable to you.

In a traditional transaction your note may be vested in your name or your company's name. But in a self-directed IRA, there is usually a bit more detail in the vesting of the note. An example of a typical IRA vested note will reference the custodian and the account number as well as the IRA holder:

ABC Custodian Company, FBO "John Investor IRA Account # 123456."

Step 3: Sign agreements which authorize the custodian to fund the note.

The custodian will typically have pre-established procedures for you to follow, and most will have the forms and agreements they need you to sign. Brokers specializing in private money lending will gladly assist you. This agreement authorizes the custodian to release the funds. Most custodians will have a checklist you can use to make sure you cover each step as the loan is originated.

Step 4: Close the transaction.

Many investors use an escrow, title company, or an attorney to close the transaction. Select a party or attorney that has worked with a self-directed custodian and it will make matters much easier.

Step 5: Send copies of the security agreements to the custodian.

Once the note is funded the IRA custodian will need to hold the actual promissory note and recorded security instrument (deed of trust, mortgage, etc.). This is similar to a conventional IRA brokerage house holding your stock certificate.

Step 6: Coordinate with the investor or servicer to send payments to the custodian.

Most investors use a third-party loan servicer to collect payments from the borrower. The servicer will likely have an authorization agreement which specifies to whom the payments are sent. Never have the interest payments sent directly to you in your name.

The investment process is simple. You simply explain how the strategy works and what is in it for the investor. Then you allow the custodian, title company and the attorneys to handle the legal end and the processing of the loan. It may be your money and your investment decisions, but before funds can be dispersed there is a process that must be followed:

1. You identify an investment that you want to make.
2. A contract is drawn up in the custodian's name and for the benefit of (FBO) your IRA account.
3. You submit an investment authorization form detailing what the money is for and where it is to be sent.
4. The custodian either approves or denies the request.
   Consult with your attorney and tax advisor to review these documents and the process entirely.

I actively loan money from my SDIRA and the process happens almost exactly as I have explained it. I have also had this conversation with dozens of investors. It is simply amazing how many people have no idea that they can do this with their own retirement accounts. They soon learn that they'll have the ultimate position--becoming the bank...and helping other people become the bank too.

Resource #5
Permanent Life Insurance, "Whole Life"

For 18 years of my life, I worked in the financial services industry. I started that career in the life insurance industry and I became a top producer and a specialist in cash value life insurance strategies. A common buzzword you need to be familiar with when discussing life insurance strategies is "infinite banking." This strategy has been gaining popularity and if you can tap into it, you will find that people are extremely willing to use their infinite banking policies to fund your deals. You should also look into setting up an infinite banking policy for yourself. (For more information visit www.themoneymultiplier.com)

One thing I can tell you is that there is more money than you could ever imagine inside cash value life insurance policies. This is one area that is often overlooked for investment capital and it is one of the best sources. The two types of insurance policies we will discuss are permanent life insurance and whole life insurance. I want you to first look at this as an asset you start to use for your own deals, then take that knowledge and apply it to other people who own whole life or permanent life insurance policies. Remember, not only are you learning how to use resources available from other people, we want to apply some of these strategies to building your own bank as well.

A typical whole life or any permanent life insurance policy is taken out for several reasons.

1. A death benefit which provides money should someone die

2. Cash accumulation that is potentially tax free, tax deferred, liquid, and guaranteed
3. Advanced strategies relating to asset protection, tax planning, and estate planning

Anyone with a permanent life insurance policy can take out a loan from that life insurance. On its surface, it's simple: you can borrow as much money as the cash value you have accumulated within the policy, tax free. Typically the money you borrow acts as collateral, and does not reduce the cash value of your policy; you don't ever have to pay back the funds, only the regular interest on the loan. However, the amount of the loan (and any accumulated interest you didn't pay) will be deducted from the final benefit your dependents receive after your death.

Let's bring this conversation full circle. We know that you can borrow money from your permanent life insurance policy and that real estate investments are what you want to invest in. Real estate provides the ultimate collateral— and if structured properly, the asset is the security for the loans. Used correctly, a life insurance loan can be the source of money you need to kick off your real estate investment strategy.

Knowing about the nature of life insurance loans leads us to a simple concept: you borrow cash value from your insurance policy and use it or loan it out; you don't have to pay back the loan amount; you save money because it's tax-free; and you allow your policy to continue accumulating interest because the loan amount remains on the account.

Over time, you can repeat this process with the newly accumulated cash value and increase your real estate portfolio. Of course you should also consider the downfalls that come with this seemingly ideal concept.

Understanding the Risks

If you have any experience in financial management, you probably know that every type of investment comes with a certain amount of risk. To say that using your life insurance to fund real estate does not have any downfalls would be dishonest. While the benefits above are undeniable, here are some risks you should understand before taking this step:

- **Loan Interest vs. Policy Interest**. Your life insurance will continue to accrue interest even against the borrowed amount. But depending on your policy, that interest may be lower than the loan interest you must pay, causing you to come away with a net negative each month. Therefore, we specifically want to use whole life policies as this rarely happens with whole life.
- **Consider the Premiums**. Once you sign a life insurance policy, you will need to pay its premiums for the life of the policy. It's tempting to think of this investment strategy as an easy way to get real estate down payments, rehab funds, or maybe fund the entire project. If you don't keep your monthly or yearly premiums up-to-date, you may find yourself in financial trouble.
- **Understanding the Details**. Especially if you are not an expert in life insurance, the many details and clauses of permanent life insurance can be difficult to understand. If you walk into a situation where the details are unclear, you may find yourself facing unexpected consequences.
- **It takes time to build**. Building cash value is not an overnight thing. It takes years and years of contributions to build a sizable cash value.

You will start to see a similar pattern with each resource I explain. You need money and investors want to earn money. That is exactly the case with whole life. Typically the average whole life policy pays an internal rate of return of around 3-5% and the typical loan interest rate is 3-6% (these rates vary greatly depending on a variety of criteria). I don't want you to get hung up on the numbers; just focus on the concept. If you need money to fund your real estate deal, you have to exceed what they earn or what it costs them to use the money. The best part about whole life is that most policy owners did not take out the life insurance policy to build and grow cash. That was a bonus to them as they wanted the life insurance protection.

Therefore, this source of money can be one you can tap at a lower interest rate than more conventional loans. I usually discuss a rate of 6-8% when talking with potential investors loaning me money from their life insurance policy. The other thing that I like is that these investors are usually more than happy to loan the money for longer periods of time than the other sources we have discussed. This may be a great place to start looking if you need funding for a rental property that you plan to hold, or a large rehab project that will take longer than 12 months.

Here are a few tips you can use to find these investors with cash value life insurance. Find some financial professionals that focus on selling life insurance and ask them to meet you for lunch. Discuss this strategy with them and ask if they know anyone who has cash value policies that would qualify for your funding needs. Then discuss what's in it for them. Coming from the financial services industry, one thing that I've learned that will highly motivate them are referrals to people who will buy what they sell or maybe this would be a good time to discuss setting up your first infinite banking policy. If you get really good at this, you will ask the advisor to get some of his co-workers together for a lunch-and-learn where you explain to them how you can increase their clients returns by using their whole life policy to fund your real estate deals. If you came up with a solid presentation showing how this works, how you protect their client's money with first-position liens, and how much you are willing to pay in interest, you will be surprised at how fast you can raise money with this one source. I always say this is an untapped source since not many people understand how to use these insurance policies to their advantage. There aren't that many people who are going after this funding source. You really should take some time and learn as much as you can about cash value life insurance, infinite banking and whole life strategies. You could literally tap into a massive source of funding if you put the time in to do so. The general public knows practically nothing about dividend-paying whole life insurance. It is all a matter of getting interested people educated about this concept.

"Every time a person buys a life insurance policy he is starting a business from scratch."-Nelson Nash

Resource #6
Hard Money Lenders

Now you're ready to learn about your Third-Party Circle: Accredited Investors and Hard Money Lenders

We have covered a few of the key sources for where money exists to fund your deals. Now let's meet some of the players who figured this out a long time ago. Hard money lenders are a great resource to tap into for funding your real estate deals. Hard money lenders tend to be a starting point for many first-time real estate investors. These loans are usually pretty expensive compared to other options but this is one of the most available sources of money when you are just starting out. Hard money loans are backed by the value of the property, and your credit history is not taken into consideration for these type of loans. Since the property itself is used as the only protection against default by the borrower, hard money loans have lower loan-to-value (LTV) ratios than regular loans.

Let talk about what these loans are, how they work and what you should expect.

A hard money loan is often issued by private investors or companies. Interest rates are generally higher than conventional commercial or residential property loans because of the greater risks associated and because of the shorter duration of the loan.

Most hard money loans are used for projects lasting from a few months to a few years. The loan amount the hard money lender can lend is determined by the ratio of loan amount divided by the value of the property. This is known as the loan to value (LTV). Many hard money lenders will lend up to 65–90% of the current value of the property.

The hard money loan market is on the rise since the 2009 mortgage crisis with the passing of the Dodd-Frank Act. The reason is due to the strict regulation put on banks and lenders in the mortgage qualification process. The Dodd-Frank and Truth in Lending Act set forth federal guidelines requiring mortgage originators, lenders, and mortgage brokers to evaluate the borrower's ability to repay the loan on primary residences or face huge fines for noncompliance. Therefore, hard money lenders only lend on business purpose or commercial loans in order to avoid the risk of the loan falling within Dodd–Frank, Truth in Lending Act, and the Home Ownership and Equity Protection Act (HOEPA) guidelines

It is important that you understand this: <u>we are talking about **commercial** lending on residential property</u>. That means these loans are issued to a business not an individual. Loans cannot be issued to you individually, they must be originated to a business or entity such as a corporation or an LLC. To stay compliant you must follow these rules and I always advise that you consult your attorney and tax professional for further guidance.

The interest rates on hard money loans are typically higher than the rates charged for traditional business loans. The interest rates could range from 10% to 18%. Despite this, such loan options are popular for their fast approvals, higher flexibility, less tedious documentation procedures and, at times, the only option for securing funds.

Hard money lenders will typically have lender fees that start high and then decline as the loan amounts get larger.

For example, some hard money lenders have a fee structure such as this:

- 2.5 points: loans between $120,000 – $249,999
- 2 points: loans between $250,000 – $499,999
- 1.5 points: loans $500,000+

These lenders work best for shorter term projects like flips, wholesale deals, or any deal that can be finished in 12 months or less.

Resource #7
Private Lenders or Private Investors

Secondary Circle: Colleagues, Friends of Friends, Personal and Professional Acquaintances. If you don't know these private lenders too well, they could be in your Third-Party Circle of Accredited Investors.

Private lenders are the ones you will want to focus your time and energy on once you have one or more deals successfully completed. This resource is one that comes with building relationships. Private lenders and the relationships you build with them will certainly be the most important to your success. Many people confuse the difference between private lenders and hard money lenders. Although they seem the same from the surface there are key differences in the two.

Private money lenders typically offer loans that are secured by a real estate asset. These loans are used to purchase a house, condo, or multifamily rental. Private money lenders can be anyone from a personal friend to an established private lending company and therefore we refer to them as "relationship-based" lenders.

Who Private Money Lenders are Right For

When I started building these relationships with private money lenders I always asked what the lender's goals were in order to determine what types of deals would be appropriate. We often find that short-term fix and flips work best (this may not be the same for you in your area) with private money lenders. However, private lenders can be great for long-term opportunities where you would rehab a rental property before refinancing into a permanent mortgage or seasoning a property before refinancing. We refer to these deals as BRRRR which stands for: Buy —Rehab — Rent — Refinance — Repeat.

Private money lenders can be a great fit for the following types of people and strategies:

- Fix-and-flippers looking to purchase, renovate, and sell a property within 1 year.
- Short-term and long-term investors who need financing quickly.
- Buy-and-hold investors looking to purchase and renovate a property before refinancing with a conventional mortgage — BRRRR.
- Long-term investors who can't qualify for a conventional mortgage, an FHA 203(k) rehab loan, or renovation/construction mortgages, but plan to refinance once they meet those qualifications.
- Long-term investors who need to season the property before the bank will refinance.

These lenders are everywhere, you just need to start looking. They can be your neighbors, a co-worker who knows you well, a family member, etc. Your job is to learn how this process works and explain the opportunity to them. Then explain where the money exists and why it's a smart investment for them to make. In other words, you must become the expert on money. You must also remember that networking is key to your success. Your network is your net worth.

Let us look at some of the fundamental things you will need to know if you are going to be the expert:

Typical Private Loan Rates, Terms & Qualifications for Private Money Lenders

Maximum Loan Amount	Up to 100% of Loan-to-Value *
	Up to 85% of After Rehab Value

	*Sometimes 100% of Loan-to-Value if the relationship exists
Minimum Required Down Payment	0-10%+ of Loan-to-Value Up to 20%+ of After Rehab Value
Interest Rates	7% - 15%
Points (Lender Fees)	0 - 10 Points
Typical Loan Term	1 - 3 Years
Time to Approval	As little as 10 minutes
Time to Funding	10 - 15 Days
Qualifications Needed for Loan Approval	Minimum Credit Score of 550 2x Personal Bank Statements

Typical Private Money Lender Loan Amount and Down Payment

Most private lenders will typically loan an amount equal to a percentage of a property's loan-to-value (LTV) ratio or its after-rehab-value (ARV). For example, hard money lenders usually offer private money loans up to:

- 100% of a property's loan-to-value (LTV)
- 80% of a property's after repair value (ARV)

A property's LTV ratio is a loan amount based on a percentage of its initial purchase price just like a conventional mortgage. A property's ARV ratio is a loan amount based on the expected fair market value (FMV) of a property after renovation.

It can be common for private lenders to issue loans based on the LTV for a property in good condition and loans based on ARV for a property in poor condition that require rehab.

When it comes to the down payment of the loan, private lenders, much like hard money lenders, usually require the borrower to have skin in the game. This protects private lenders and hard money lenders from default. It's therefore common for private money borrowers to invest their own cash when working with private lenders, up to:

- 10% or more of LTV
- 20% or more of ARV
- renovation expenses and closing costs

Many times, you can negotiate a draw schedule into the terms of the loan which would reimburse you for money you spent on the renovations after the work has been done. We do this all of the time. It allows us to be doing more deals at the same time because it frees up our personal capital once the work is done. It's important to understand that this only happens after you have built a trusted relationship with the private lenders.

Private Money Lender Interest Rates, Costs, & Fees

The payments on a private money loan are almost always interest-only payments. This means that you, as the borrower will pay monthly interest throughout the term of the loan and then make full repayment at the end of the loan. Some lenders charge prepayment penalties if the loan is paid off before the due date so it's a good idea to ask if one exists.

Monthly payments are not amortized like a conventional mortgage. However, while the interest rates on a private money loan might be higher than when compared to a conventional mortgage, the monthly payments might be less because they do not include principal payments.

This makes private money loans a great option for flippers looking to reduce their holding costs and expenses while they prepare a property for sale. It also makes private money loans advantageous for buy-and-hold or BRRRR investors since the monthly payments are lower while they look to refinance with conventional mortgage alternatives.

Be aware that private lenders can also charge fees, known as "points," between 0% – 10%.

As I mentioned earlier, this is all about the relationship and the terms can vary greatly based on the relationships you build. I am trying to give you some basic guidelines so you are familiar with these terms if they are brought up in your discussions or so that you can ask the right questions when negotiating terms.

Private Money Lender Loan Term and Approval Time

Private money loans can have terms that range anywhere from 1 month to 3 years or more. However, when a borrower works with private lenders just like hard money lenders, loan terms are between 1 – 3 years. Most hard money lenders try to keep their loans to a 1-year term. Hard money lenders also might have prepayment penalties, which force a borrower to make all the agreed monthly interest payments.

The approval and funding times of a private money loan are typically as follows:

- Prequalification: as little as 10 minutes
- Funding: as quick as 10 – 15 days

This allows investors to compete with all-cash borrowers and close on a house quickly.

Private Money Lender Loan Qualifications

Private money lenders generally have standardized loan qualifications for their private money loans. A national hard money lender will expect to see the following during prequalification:

- Credit Score of 550+
- 2 – 3 Months of Bank Statements
- Property Location & Expected Purchase Price

If the borrower is seeking a hard money rehab loan, hard money lenders will require the following 3 items in order to approve and fund the renovation budget:

- Details on your experience and prior projects you have done
- Detailed renovation scope of work
- Contractor bids and independent contractor agreements if you have them

Afterward, borrowers are expected to provide their lenders with the following in order to approve the funding:

- Purchase contract stipulating the agreed upon purchase price and terms of sale and all necessary documents (varies state by county / state)

In our personal experience there is no limit to the number of private loans a borrower can take out. Further, hard money and private lender loans can either finance a house in good condition or finance the purchase and renovations of a house in poor condition. It all depends on the price you bought the property for. Therefore, I will keep saying <u>the money in this business is always made on the buy, not the sell.</u>

Resource #8
Banks and Community Banks

I saved this one for last because you will typically start with private funding then you will use bank funding as a secondary funding to replace private funding. We use community banks for our rentals and especially our BRRRR strategies. The bank funding is so vitally important to our success because it allows us to pay off our private investors when we decide to keep a property as a rental or if we get into trouble on a renovation that takes longer than anticipated. The secret to using banks is being prepared for your interview and building a relationship. I will discuss the preparation part in **Chapter 6: The Perfect Loan Proposal**, and we will discuss bank strategies more in **Chapter 8, The Second Phase of Financing.** It is important that you start to look for a strong community bank to build a relationship with. This will be an integral part of your success in real estate when you move into rentals and are looking for longer hold strategies.

I cannot stress the importance of using community banks instead of commercial banks. When you're applying for a mortgage with a community bank you understand that the loan is a commercial loan, even though it is a residential property. Commercial real estate loans mean you will be borrowing in the name of your corporation or LLC not your personal name. Community banks are your best bet because it is easier to build a relationship with these banks.

The loans you will be taking out from them are portfolio loans. Community Banks keep these in house and don't sell them on the secondary market.

You will usually be granted a bit more leeway than you'd get from national banks. There is something to be said about having a strong relationship with a community bank. Decisions are made quickly and the board of directors can approve a loan in two to three weeks, or at their next monthly board meeting. Commercial and national banks do not operate this way and you will find yourself jumping through hoops if you try and do this with a large commercial institution.

Here are some important steps to building a relationship with a community bank. First, you need to find the right one for your particular needs. Here are some ways I found the community banks we use:

1. Ask for Referrals

If a bank has lent to another real estate investor who is doing what you are doing, then why wouldn't they lend to you? At the very least, your odds are better. The very first place to start when looking for a bank, is to ask around. Start by asking any real estate investors that you know. Then, go to your local Real Estate Investors Association (REIA) meeting. Rub shoulders with other investors and ask them who they are getting loans from. I've never met a single investor at these events too shy to answer this question. There's no reason to limit this question just to real estate investors. Be open about what you do. Always be asking for referrals.

2. Networking

While investors are great for bank leads, another place to look is by networking *where bankers network*. For example, I found one of our lenders at a BNI meeting, which is a networking meeting that meets all over the world. Many of the members in these groups are bankers. Most bankers know who is lending and what appetite those banks have at that time. Other places you could consider are chamber of commerce meetings, property managers and management companies, and alike meetings. Most bankers like to network, and happy hour networking events are perfect places to meet these lenders.

3. Don't Be Afraid to Meet with Several Community Banks

Pick up the phone, pull up your search engine and type in "community banks near me." Then start calling them. Ask to speak with someone in the commercial lending department. Then just tell them what you are looking for:

"We buy single family houses and small multifamily properties in [these areas]. We then fix them up and rent them out. We are looking for a bank that is willing to refinance our properties at 75-80% of their as-complete appraised value. Is this something you would be interested in?"

I would then set up a meeting and try to build some rapport to make sure we are a good fit to do business together.

After that, I would submit a perfect loan proposal *(see chapter 6 for this)*. Then I would discuss your willingness to move your current accounts and get the relationship started.

4. Look the Part and Be Prepared When You Meet with the Bank

When you meet with the bank you want to be fully prepared. You will want to dress nicely and look professional. More importantly you will need to have all your information prepared and ready. It's also helpful to have a deal to discuss when you go. Don't ask for something from the bank without being prepared. You can ask basic questions when you call to be sure the community bank will lend under the terms you need. You also need to respect the bankers time; time is money. I have created an entire process for dealing with banks and lenders. It's a step-by-step guide that will give lenders everything they could ask for on the first meeting which saves them time, makes you look professional and knowledgeable, and the most important part is it makes the lender want to do business with you. People want to do business with people who are prepared and who don't waste their time. The guide I just mentioned will be covered in Chapter 6.

In conclusion, it is important to understand that each one of these resources will take time and effort. You do not need to do all of them. I firmly believe that to be successful in anything, you must first learn, then you must apply that knowledge immediately. Whatever golden nuggets you take out of this chapter I need you to take action and apply what you have learned.

Chapter 3
Finding the Deal

This is one of my favorite topics to teach. The **one thing** you *must* become good at before you can ever apply 90% of the information in this booklet, is finding the DEAL. <u>Once you find the deal, the money will follow</u>. No deal? No money. This is the single most important aspect for your success as a real estate investor.

I am going to give you my 10 Tips to Finding Lucrative Off-Market Deals. You will notice that is says *lucrative* off-market deals. I have spent years developing and teaching people the ways my team and I find properties with a lot of 'meat on the bone' on a consistent basis in any market. I will say that we have found a few diamonds in the rough on the MLS and from realtors, but almost every deal we do is a deal no one else knew about. We don't just find good deals —we create them.

If there was one thing I could teach you that would instantly generate profitable real estate deals, I certainly would. However, that simply does not exist. What it really takes is doing several things consistently and persistently. I will also say this, you had better get good at the formula I give you in the next chapter! This formula will help you determine the maximum offer you can make on a property. It is not hard to go out there and find potential properties... but you'll pay too much for them. Anyone can do that, and they will lose money most of the time. The money you make in this business is on the buy, not the sell. The market will always determine the sale price, not anything you do to make the property a masterpiece.

The Private Money Guide: Real Estate Edition

10 TIPS TO FINDING LUCRATIVE OFF MARKET DEALS

1. Look for distressed properties in the areas you know the market best i.e) where you live/grew up

2. Knock on those distressed property doors and ask to speak with owner or get in touch with landlord

3. Ask the neighbors questions about the property or of the owners whereabouts or schedule

4. Call tax assessor to find the mailing address and send owner a letter inquiring about property

5. Connect with a real estate agent / broker whom specializes in REO, Foreclosures, Short-Sales and Bankruptcies

6. Look for estate sale signs and speak with the person in charge

7. Connect with an estate attorney, many families will soon look to list the house after a death

8. Visit the auctions and be chatty with the ones bidding on houses--they often need to unload properties, too.

9. Stagnant for sale by owner properties

10. Post an ad on social mediums expressing interest in purchasing houses for cash

Now that you have the 10 ways to go out and find deals, it is important to apply this knowledge right away. In our business we have gotten so busy that we have had to refine how we implement these 10 tips. In the beginning, we struggled to find deals; today, the deals just keep coming because we have built systems to handle our growth. When you start to build and scale your business, you will also have to find ways to systematize these processes. You will have to hire people or find other companies that specialize in these methods. You will also begin to develop relationships and word will spread that you are an active buyer. The deals will start to pour in as your credibility begins to grow. If you apply the concepts in this booklet you will eventually have enough money available to fund many deals at the same time and then new challenges will arise from that. You may just decide to be the bank and allow other people to do what you have learned to do. No matter what path you decide to take, the principles in this booklet will help you catapult your business in ways you do not yet know.

Chapter 4
Analysis & Strategy

When you find a subject property you'll have to analyze the figures to see if it's a possible deal. The first step is the most time sensitive. first figure out how much to offer for the deals you find. This can be difficult since you will very rarely have every single piece of information you need to make a buying decision...*and* it can also be nerve-wracking because you have to make this decision <u>very quickly</u> **or you may lose out.** It's the ones that move quickly and accurately that have massive success. That does not mean we are going to just wing it. I have two formulas that my team and I have created. This is a simple template that allows you to come up with a max offer. This formula is used on every single deal that we make an offer on. It works at auctions, on the phone and in person, and the digital template version takes about 30 seconds. If you want to download the digital template, it's available on www.flipoutacademy.com/shop for a few bucks.

Here is the information you will need to know for the formula to work:

1. The ARV (after rehab value) of the property
2. The rehab costs to finish the property and have it ready to sell or rent
3. The cost of borrowing money and estimated closing and carry costs

Here is the manual version of the short form *Max Offer Formula*:

*Average Closing Costs = 3-6% "Seller Concession" = 2-4%

On every property we intend to flip in Western New York, we try to make approximately:

$10 - 20k on a property in the $100k's

$20 - 30k on a property in the $200k's

$30 - 40k on a property in the $300k's

$40 - 50k on a property in the $400k's

We typically purchase properties anywhere between $40k to $400k

Here is an example of what a max allowable offer might look like:

After Repair Price	$110,000
Discount (10-15%)	$-10,000
Repairs (30%)	$-30,000
Profit (20%)	$-20,000
MAX Allowable Offer & Purchase Price	$ 50,000
Put Repair Costs back in +	$ 30,000
Loan Amount	$ 80,000

MAX ALLOWABLE OFFER LONG FORM

CMA: Comparable Market Analysis: Comparison of prices of similar houses, with similar square footage in the same geographical location. We will use this to determine the property value for a buyer or a seller.

Critical data:

- Recent sales in the area (30 - 180 days)

- ½ mile radius for urban areas, 1 mile radius for suburban locations, and 5 mile radius for rural areas
- structure is within 200-ish sq ft
- pull 5 comps with similar design and acreage.

If criteria do not meet initial analysis, move in 90-day increments up to 1 year or up to a one-mile radius (rural properties up to 2 miles)

Running Numbers: (Maximum Allowable Offer)

- ARV (After Repair Value)
- Less Repair Costs
    - Subtract Purchase Costs (1%)
    - Subtract Holding Costs (3%)
    - Subtract Sales Costs (3%)
    - Subtract Maximum Acceptable Profit (20%)
    - Subtract "Fudge Factor" (3-5% of sale price)

Putting it into perspective. Here is an example:

After Repair Value	$ 130,000
15% Discount (10-15%)	$ - 10,000
Our Sale Price	$ - 120,000
Repair Costs (min. 3 estimates)	$ - 30,000
1% Purchase Costs	$ - 1,200 (= $120,000 x1%)

3% Holding Costs	$ - 3,600
3% Closing Costs	$ - 3,600
20% My Profit	$ - 26,000 (= 20% of $130,000)
3% (oops) Fudge Factor	$ - 3,600
Maximum Allowable Offer	$ 52,000 (+/-) 10-15% variance
Assignment Fee (buyer)	$ - 5,000
Max Allowable Offer IF ASSIGNED	$ 47,000

*Average Closing Costs = 3-6%. "Seller Concession" = 2-4%.

We have two versions of this formula. The long form version is for deals you will have more time and more information to come up with your offer. The short form is for deals you need to come up with an offer on the fly or in a short period of time. This business is getting more and more competitive all the time. As more people enter the business you will need to master these formulas and refine your skills, so that you will beat them to the deals and to ultimately presenting your offer.

When I started in this business I missed out on many amazing opportunities because I was scared to make a decision. Fear costs me hundreds of thousands of dollars. Let me tell you about the one thing that changed it all for me. In 2009 I was struggling like so many others; the recession had hit me hard. I was in the middle of my first plaza development, my financial advisory business had come to a screeching halt, Phatman dropped 30% overnight and I was working harder than I had ever worked in my life and barely making ends meet. I was looking for that opportunity that would get me out of that mess. I remember this vividly and I will never forget the moment. This broker I knew brought me a deal. It was three-unit apartment building in downtown Buffalo, NY. It was cash flow positive, the area was on the verge of exploding, and it was only $175,000. The broker kept telling me that this was the deal of a lifetime and I completely agreed. However, I started thinking, "What if this area doesn't boom?" "What if I can't find the money to close on the deal?" What if a tenant moves out and I can't afford the bills?" Fear started to get the best of me. After weeks had went by, I simply ignored the broker's calls and went on with my struggles and life in general. Three years later I was driving down that street and I saw the property... but, something was very different; the area was booming, and the property looked amazing—it had been completely transformed! I did some research and what I found out made me sick to my stomach. Had I bought that property it would have been worth $400,000 a short three years later. Fast forward again to today, that property would be worth almost a million dollars. You see, I allowed fear to talk me out of almost a million dollars. At that moment I made a decision, not some wishy-washy decision but a firm decision. I decided that _I would never again let fear stop me from achieving the life I want._

That leads me to the next important lesson: When you are analyzing the deal, it is important to determine more than one strategy. This will allow you to fine-tune your calculations and sometimes the numbers will fluctuate on the price you are willing to pay determining what strategy you're weighing in on. For example, if the numbers don't work as a flip, you may think about holding on the property either short or long term.

Here are a few strategies I use in my business:

1. Wholesaling: this includes assignment, double-close, wholesaling to another investor
2. Fix and Flip: buy, rehab and resell to an end buyer
3. BRRRR: buy, rehab, rent, refinance, repeat

4. Multi-family rentals (some for low income tenants or whom are on assistance because it's important to stay diverse)

Every deal I look at has several potential strategies:

Strategy 1.) I will always try to assign or wholesale the property first. The way I look at it, if I can make a profit quickly with very little effort I will always do that. Even if I give up a good deal, I know I will find another one.

Strategy 2.) If I was unable to find a buyer to wholesale the deal to I will always look at a fix and flip strategy.

Strategy 3.) Sometimes when you get into a deal, it becomes very clear that you should hold the property and rent it. This determination can be made at the very beginning, in the middle, or in the end when you cannot sell it.

Strategy 4.) This is a strategy I use when markets are declining or at a low point such as (2008-2012). This includes buying multi-family rental properties.

The rental strategy has been our go-to strategy since 2018 because the profit margins for fix and flips have been getting tighter and properties have been selling slower. The BRRRR strategy just seems to make the most sense in our market. Banks have been eager to lend on renovated properties with solid rents. Properties have been appreciating which makes it hard to sell something for less profit just because the buyers are being difficult. We prefer to hold the asset, collect rent, and wait for the appreciation.

Whatever strategy you decide on will depend on the market you are in and your personal preference. Just make sure you do the analysis on a few strategies in case one backfires. It's always smart to have exit strategies. Markets will change, seasons will change and your deal may not go exactly as planned. If you do the homework beforehand, you will be prepared to handle almost anything that happens.

Chapter 5
Structuring the Deal

In this chapter, you will learn how to structure your deal so that it looks professional. This will be essential when it comes to presenting the deal to a lender. This is a lesson in marketing. The more organized and professional your deal looks, the more experienced and professional you will look to a potential lender. Structuring will also provide the lender with necessary information required to make a fast decision. You certainly do not want to put a property under contract and then find out you cannot get the necessary funds to close. This is not good for your business or for your reputation. All you need to do is present the analysis and necessary information about your deal in a very organized fashion. This is also an important step that will be required in the next chapter when building your perfect loan proposal.

This is very simple to do and we have created a system in our business that allows us to quickly structure a deal. Here is the information you will need to prepare:

Step #1

The Deal - This is your analysis of the deal. Specifics about the property, how many bedrooms and bathrooms, sq. footage, type of property, desired strategy and the potential profit or rent roll.

Step #2

The Scope of Work - This can be your scope of work outlining the detailed renovations you plan to do, or you can include contractor quotes to show the costs and specifics of the work to be done.

Step #3

Comparable Sales - This will be used to support your ARV and show the fair market value. You can pull your own comps by using Zillow, Trulia or Realtor.com but we suggest asking a realtor or broker to help you create a Comparative Market Analysis (CMA) or a Broker's Price Opinion (BPO).

Step #4

The Appraisal - This is not required, but it will strengthen your deal to the lender or buyer. There are two types of appraisals. An *as-is appraisal* will tell you what a property is worth in its present condition. The one we commonly used to support our ARV is called an as-complete appraisal. The as-complete appraisal will give you a value based on the scope of work you provide the appraiser. In other words, this will be an accurate representation of what the bank will value the property at. This is important because it allows you to run the analysis for the BRRRR strategy by giving you a close estimate of the amount the bank will lend on. An appraisal will cost between $300 to as much as a few thousand dollars for multi-family properties. It's a small price to pay to predict the future value of your property.

Step #5

Photos - You want to include photos showing all the rooms and mechanicals of the property. It is important to label the photos, so the lender knows what room they are looking at. You may also want to add a *Google Maps* link to the street scene so the investor can see where the property's location.

Check out how we incorporate a deal kit for each property:

Chapter 5: Structuring the Deal

02 SPEC SHEET

Name: **John Smith**
Company: **Smith Realty, LLC**
Phone Number: **716-555-1212**
Address: **45 Main St, Buffalo, NY**

PROPERTY SPECIFICATION SHEET

PROPERTY INFORMATION

Property Address:	123 Anystreet	City, State / Province, Zip / Postal Code:	Buffalo, NY 14222
Servicer Loan #:		School District:	Buffalo
Type of Property:	■ SFR ☐ Townhouse ☐ Condo ☐ Duplex ☐ Triplex ☐ 4-Plex ☐ Other		
BPO Date:		REO #:	

NEIGHBORHOOD ANALYSIS

Location:	☐ Urban	■ Suburban	☐ Rural
Neighborhood Condition:	■ Excellent	☐ Good	☐ Fair
Demand/Supply:	■ Shortage	☐ In Balance	☐ Over Supply
Property Values:	■ Increasing	☐ Stable	☐ Declining
Investor Owned %:	20	Owner Occupied %:	80
New Construction:	☐ Yes ■ No	If Yes, # of units:	
Estimated Marketing Time:	45 Days	# Of properties for sale:	N/A

SUBJECT PROPERTY DESCRIPTION

Property Style	Bed	Bath	Age	Sq. Ft.	Lot Sq. Ft.	Basement	# Car Garage	Condition
SFR	4	2	1957	1,606	10,880	None/Slab	1 car	Fair

Septic:	N/A	Well Water:	N/A	Oil / Propane:	N/A
Heating Type:	Forced Air	Flood Zone:	N/A	Agricultural Zone:	N/A
HOA / Age 55+ Restriction:	N/A				
Positive attributes of the subject property:	Large house, California Ranch, High Demand Area, Amazing Neighborhood				
Negative aspects of the subject property:	No Basement				

ESTIMATED AGE OF MECHANICALS

Windows:	Replace Some	HWT:	Replace	Furnace:	Good- Have Cleaned
Roof:	Minor repair needed			Electrical Wiring & Box:	Needs updating
A/C:	None			Plumbing:	Some copper/ pex

COMPARABLE SALES ANALYSIS

	Address	Dist.	Cond.	BR/BA	Age	Sq. Ft.	Lot SF	Gar.	Bsmt.	List Price	Sale Price	Sale Date	DOM
1.	79 Bonita Dr.	.2	Good	4/2	1947	1,730	6,396	1.5 car	None	$	$		Pending
2.	77 Alys Dr. West	.2	Good	3/2	1956	1,650	22,620	None	None	$	$	8/17/17	6
3.	160 Cheryl Lane	.3	Good	4/1	1958	1,652	7,933	1 car	None	$	$	10/16/17	391

Please compare properties to the subject, and note if the comparable property is superior, inferior, or equal to the subject property.

1. ARV is determined by multiplying the Avg. Sold Price Per Sq./Ft. of the 3 comps by the Sq./Ft. Of our property
2. The Avg. Sold Price Per Sq./Ft. of the 3 comps is $84.46 making our ARV $135,810.81
3.

Call or Email Today!
716.800.1892
Chris@Lcstrategicrealty.com

FLIPOUT ACADEMY

Chapter 5: Structuring the Deal

03 SPEC SHEET

RECOMMENDED REPAIRS

REPAIRS:		COST OF REPAIRS:
1.	Flooring Throughout	$4,000.00
2.	Rear Roof Repairs and Exterior Paint	$4,200.00
3.	Electric update, HWT replacement and Furnace clean	$2,500.00
4.	Doors, Sliders and windows in need of replacement	$2,200.00
5.	Redo Fireplace	$800.00
6.	Rear Bath Redo	$3,000.00
7.	Main bath redo	$3,500.00
8.	Kitchen Renovation	$8,000.00
9.	Lighting budget	$1,200.00
10.	Paint interior	$2,500.00
11.		$
12.		$
	TOTAL REPAIRS:	$31,900.00

MARKETING STRATEGY

Type of deal structure:	■ Wholesale ☐ Assignment ☐ Double Close ☐ Retail ☐ Other
Explain deal structure:	This is a wholesale deal
ARV (After Rehab Value) / Suggested List Price:	$135,810.81
Probable Sales Price (recommendation of 10% lower than ARV):	No discount due to high demand area
Purchase Contract Price (assignment deals):	$
Assignment Fee: $	Wholesale / Double Price: $75,000 Retail Price: $
Marked this asset As-Is or Repaired:	■ As Is ☐ Repaired
Explanation for As-Is or Repaired:	Buyer responsible for any and all repairs
Who is the most likely Buyer for this asset?	Investor, Flipper

DEAL RUN DOWN (Summary of Your Pricing Strategy & Profit Margin)

ARV (After Rehab Value) / Suggested List Price:	$135,810.81
Minus the 10% discount (this is optional and a value of 0 may be inserted):	$0.00
Minus the Estimated Rehab Cost:	$31,900.00
Minus other accumulated expenses:	$77,632.50
Please explain other expenses:	Purchase Price $75,000, Closing Costs $2632.50
PROJECTED DEAL PROFIT (The final sum left from the ARV):	$26,278.31
Comments:	This ARV is conservative based on the comps. There are houses that have sold for more but we wanted to showcase conservative numbers

COMPANY CONTACT INFORMATION

Agent		Company	
Address:		Telephone #:	
Fax:		E-Mail:	

Call or Email Today!
716.800.1892
Chris@Lcstrategicrealty.com

FLIPOUT ACADEMY

The Private Money Guide: Real Estate Edition

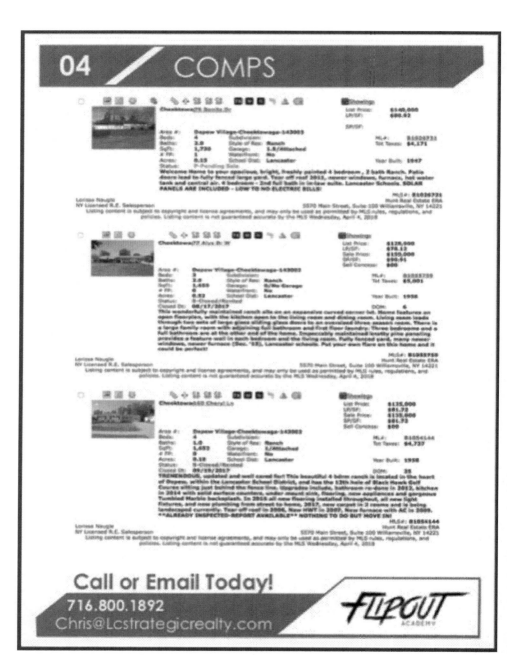

Chapter 5: Structuring the Deal

Chapter 5: Structuring the Deal

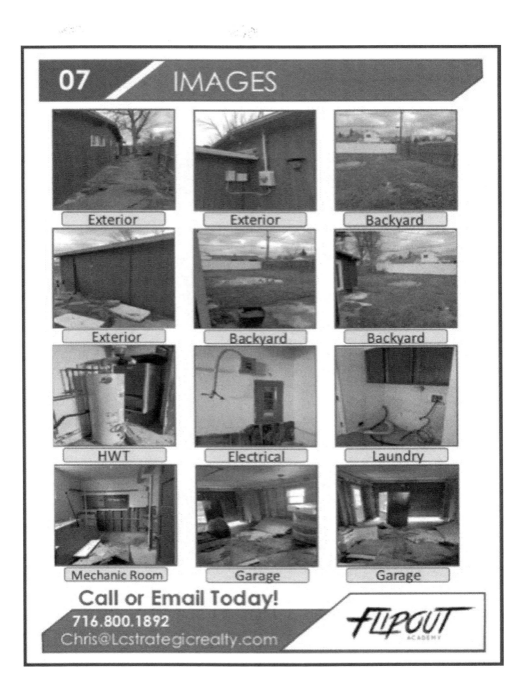

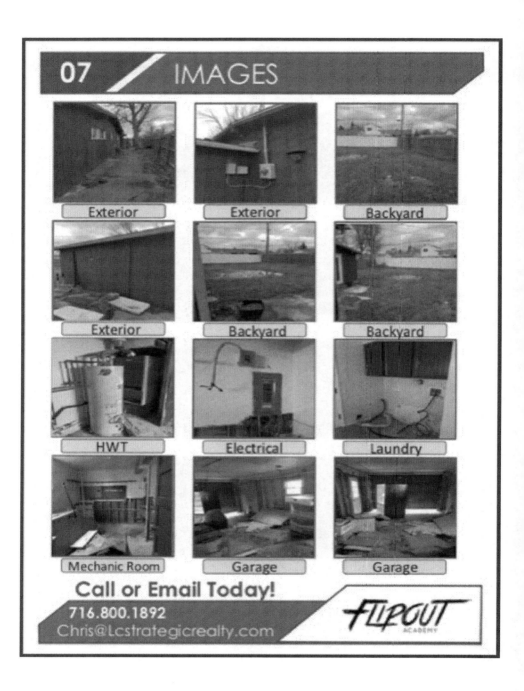

Chapter 5: Structuring the Deal

Chapter 6
The Perfect Loan Proposal

Want to get a lender to fund your deal? You will need to be prepared for everything the lender could (and will) ask for, ...and then some. Here is a template to use that will help you build a funding proposal that will impress any lender. This works well with banks, hard money lenders, private equity investors, or anyone you ask to fund your real estate deal.

Do not give them the opportunity to say, "No." Being unorganized or unprofessional will throw up a big red flag. Therefore, all you need to do is follow these steps and you will eliminate almost every question a lender could have about you, your business, and your deal.

There are rules to follow when creating and presenting this to any lender.

First, you will need some supplies to create this proposal. Get a new, professional-looking 1/2" 3-ring binder (not a previously used or cheap-looking one)

- 3-hole punch
- Quality paper and a like-new ink cartridge
- Highlighter
- 3-ring binder divider sheets (we like the clear plastic ones with the colored tabs and the table of contents included)

Sections for your Perfect Loan Proposal:

1. **Cover Page:** with your a.) business name b.) logo c.) one sentence that sums up what you and your business do and d.) a title for this proposal. i.e.: "Real Estate Investor" or "Loan Proposal"

2. **Table of Contents:** List out each section and what is included

3. **Description of You and Your Business:** We call it "The Credibility Builder," which tells the lender what you do and why you are different. Your "*who, what, why, and where you buy.*" What is your hook and why should they look at you as someone who is credible, knowledgeable and lendable? *Include a picture of yourself with a professional background so the lender can associate you with the proposal.*

4. **The Deal:** ...and all the specifics about your deal. Don't forget to include the scope of work if it's a rehab, potential profit if it's a fix and flip, rental income projections/pro forma if you are renting, and any other important information relating to your deal.

5. **Comparable Sales:** or a 3rd party appraisal (as-complete appraisal if it's a rehab)

6. **Corporate Documents and Articles of Incorporation and EIN Number**: This just shows the lender that you are a legitimate business. Most lenders will not lend to an individual.

7. **Personal Financial Statements:** This is commonly known as a PFS. This is the most important part and it must be precise. (see template included)

8. **Statements:** for all the assets you listed in the PFS. You MUST include statements for all investment accounts, bank statements, retirement accounts, business interest, etc. These are essential to prove that your figures are accurate.

9. **Other Real Estate:** (if applicable) include an extra page(s) showcasing your portfolio.

10. **3 Years of Personal and Business Tax Returns:** (This is a MUST so start digging for those returns). If they don't fit in the binder just include a page that says 3 years tax returns available upon request.

11. **Credit Reports with Scores:** Search online for free credit reports. We recommend printing out all three (Equifax, TransUnion & Experian)

PERSONAL FINANCIAL STATEMENT TEMPLATE
Statement Date:

Personal Information

Name:		SSN:	
Address:		Birthdate:	
City, State Zip:		Dependents:	
Home Telephone:		Business Telephone:	

Section I

ASSETS		LIABILITIES
1. Cash on Hand & in Banks		Notes Due to Banks
2. Cash Value of Life Insurance		Notes Due to Relatives & Friends
3. U.S. Gov. Securities		23 Notes Due to Others
4. Other Marketable Securities		
5. Notes & Accounts Receivable - Good		Accounts & Bills Payable
6. Other Assets Readily Convertible to Cash - Itemize		
7 Other Assets		
8 Other Assets		Unpaid Income Taxes Due - Federal State
9 Other Assets		
10 TOTAL CURRENT ASSETS	$0.00	26 Other Unpaid Taxes & Interest
11 Real Estate Owned Mortgages & Contracts Owned		27 Loans on Life Insurance Policies
Notes & Accounts Receivable - Doubtful		28 Contract Accounts Payable
14 Notes Due from Relatives & Friends		Cash Rent Owed
15 Other Securities - Not Readily Marketable		Other Liabilities Due within 1 Year - Itemize
16 Personal Property		
17 Other Assets - Itemize		
18 Other Assets		
19 Other Assets	$0.00	
20 TOTAL ASSETS		32 TOTAL CURRENT LIABILITIES $0.00
		33 Real Estate Mortgage Payable
		34 Liens & Assessments Payable
		35 Other Debts - Itemize
		36 TOTAL LIABILITIES $0.00

Chapter 6: The Perfect Loan Proposal

	37 Net Worth (Total Assets - Total Liabilities) $0.00 38 TOTAL LIABILITIES & NET WORTH $0.00

ANNUAL INCOME		ESTIMATE OF ANNUAL EXPENSES	
Salary, Bonuses & Commissions		Income Taxes	
Dividends & Interest		Other Taxes	
Rental & Lease Income (Net)		Insurance Premiums	
Other Income - Itemize		Mortgage Payments	
Other Persons Salary, Bonuses & Commissions		Rent Payable	
Other Income of Other Person - Itemize		Other Expenses	
Total	$0.00	Total	$0.00

GENERAL INFORMATION	CONTINGENT LIABILITIES
Are any Assets Pledged? No Yes	As Endorser, Co-maker or Guarantor- Yes
Are you a Defendant in any No Yes Suits or Legal Actions? (Explain)	On Leases or Contracts Legal Claims
Have you ever been No Yes declared Bankrupt in the last 10 years? (Explain)	Federal - State Income Taxes Other -

Section II
A CASH IN BANKS AND NOTES DUE TO BANKS

Name of Bank	Type of Account	Type of Ownership	On Deposit	Notes Due Banks	COLLATERAL (If any) & Type of Ownership
Cash on Hand					
TOTALS			$0.00	$0.00	

The Private Money Guide: Real Estate Edition

SECTION II (Continued)
B LIFE INSURANCE (List only those Policies that you own)

Company	Face of Policy	Cash Surrender Value	Policy Loan from Insurance Co.	Other Loans Policy as Collateral	BENEFICIARY
TOTALS		$0.00	$0.00		

SECURITIES OWNED

Face Value-Bonds No. of Shares Stock	Indicate those Not Registered in Your	Type of Ownership	COST	Market Value U.S. Gov. Sec.	Market Value Marketable Sec.	MARKET VALUE Not Readily Marketable SECURITIES	Amount Pledged to Secured Loans
TOTALS				$0.00	$0.00	$0.00	

NOTES AND ACCOUNTS RECEIVABLE (Money Payable or Owed to You Individually-Indicate by a X if Others have an Ownership Interest)

MAKER/DEBTOR	X	When Due	Original Amount	Balance Due Good Accounts	Balance Due Doubtful Accounts	Bal. Due Notes Rel. & Friends	Security (if any)
TOTALS				$0.00	$0.00	$0.00	

Chapter 6: The Perfect Loan Proposal

REAL ESTATE OWNED (Indicate by an X if Others have an Ownership Interest)						MORTGAGE OR CONTRACT PAYABLE			
TITLE IN NAME OF	Description & Location	X	Date Acquired	Original Cost	Present Value of Real Estate	Amount of Ins. Carried	Bal. Due	Payment	Maturity	To Whom Payable
TOTAL				$0.00	TOTAL	$0.00			

F MORTGAGES AND CONTRACTS OWNED (Indicate by "A" if Others have an Ownership Interest)

Contract	Mortgage	X	Maker Name	Maker Address	Property Covered	Start Date	Payment	Maturity	Balance Due
TOTALS									$0.00

Chapter 6: The Perfect Loan Proposal

G PERSONAL PROPERTY (Indicate by a X if Others have an Ownership Interest)

DESCRIPTION	X	Date When New	Cost When New	Value Today	Balance Due	To Whom Payable
TOTAL				$0.00		

H NOTES (Other than Bank, Mortgage and Insurance Company Loans)

PAYABLE TO	Other Obligors (if any)	When Due	Notes Due To Rel. & Friends	Notes Due Others (Not Banks)	Accounts & Bills Payable	Contracts Payable	COLLATERAL (if any)
TOTALS			$0.00	$0.00	$0.00	$0.00	

For the purpose of procuring credit from time to time, I/We furnish the foregoing as a true and accurate statement of my/our financial condition.

The goal is to create a digital version and a concrete version that you can bring with you. Below is an example of what it should look like:

Chapter 6: The Perfect Loan Proposal

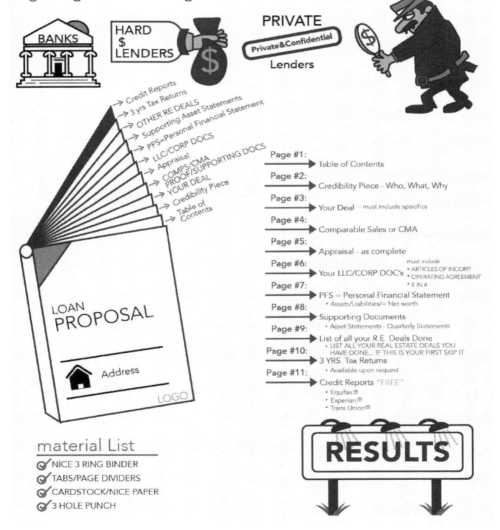

Chapter 7
Execution

You…

- Found the property
- Analyzed the deal
- Chose what strategy is best for you (or your end buyer)
- Structured the deal
- Financed the property (maybe even the rehab portion)
- Renovated and managed the project with the use of a draw-schedule
- Executed your strategy to sell it, refinance it, rent it, or leverage it
- Now you have to repeat the process

In this business it is so easy to fall victim to paralysis by analysis. I see this every day with people we meet at our events. We live in a world where knowledge is everywhere. We also live in a time where we know the price of everything and the value of nothing. The issue with that is people spend weeks, months, and even years researching everything, watching podcasts and gathering all this information, yet they never apply that knowledge. I can promise you this, if you don't apply knowledge in a systematic manner you will NEVER get results. Application of knowledge is what gets results. Let me prove this to you right now. Most of us took a foreign language in high school, i.e.) Spanish, French, Latin, etc. and we spent years in a classroom learning this language. Then we went off to college or into the workforce and we stopped applying what we were taught, and we never practiced. Fast forward to today—if you took a language (other than English) do you still speak that language today? Your answer is probably no or not very well.

The execution is what matters. I summarized everything I have been telling you in a systematic manner so that you can begin to apply this information in order to get results. If you don't know this by now, the results are MONEY.

Step 1:

You have to get over your fears and get into the proper mindset. You have to learn that you don't know, what you don't know. Hopefully, you learned that money is not a barrier and that it exists everywhere, if you know where to look, and how to use the different resources. This was found in Chapters 1 & 2 if you need to go back and review this.

Step 2:

You need to find a deal. It is great that you now know where all the money is and how to tap into those resources. However, if you don't have the deal under contract or in your control you have nothing to discuss. This is the most important thing in this business. I'll repeat it again, "the money in this business is made on the buy, not the sell." You need to learn and master this and you need to become a master at finding lucrative off-market deals. This is not difficult, but it requires you to be extremely persistent and consistent. This *sounds* easy, but 80% of you will never master this skill set. The reason for this will be lack of effort and nothing else. Start working the funnels and start researching all the ways to find deals that I discussed in the **10 Tips**. Once you have a deal it is time to move to the next step. Can't find a deal yourself? That's totally ok. Don't be afraid to pay an assignment fee to a wholesaler, but make sure their numbers are accurate. Do your own due diligence.

Step 3:

Now that you have identified the deal, you're ready to run the numbers. This is a critical part of the process because you do not want to make any mistakes and miss something. The analysis is what will allow you to make sound decisions and not overpay for the property. The other thing this analysis will do for you is help you determine a strategy for the property. Is it a fix and flip? Will you wholesale it? Or maybe the numbers are perfect for a rental. Analysis will solidify all those ideas you have about the property and the end result will tell you whether or not you have a good deal. Whatever the end result is, just remember this, never force a deal when the numbers don't make sense. It's a formula that does not lie and the only one that can screw it up is you.

Step 4:

Now that you have ran the numbers and you have identified a few possible strategies that will work, it's time to structure this deal in order to present it properly. The structuring process is multifaceted; it can be used when presenting your deal to another investor to wholesale or assign, or, it can be used when presenting the deal to a bank or a private lender. It can even be layered with the perfect loan proposal materials to make a powerful marketing kit that will impress even the most experienced investors. This step is all about putting your deal on paper in a systematic fashion so that all the positive aspects of your deal are right in front of the reviewer. The specifics you should include are:

- information about the deal
- the comparable sales that support the ARV
- the numbers showing the potential profit or passive income and return on investment
- detailed photos that accurately show the deal

I like to structure my deals so that an investor across the world could review my deal and make a buying decision within 30 minutes to an hour. By the way that statement is a true story; I assigned a deal to an investor in Dubai without him ever seeing the property. The deal was structured so well that he was able to make a buying decision in 45 minutes because I gave him all the information he needed to make that decision and I eliminated all of his potential questions with factual data. This step is covered in detail in chapter 5.

Step 5:

We are almost at the point where we can start presenting our deal to find the money we need. This next step is called the perfect loan proposal. This is where we take all the analysis and we build a complete loan proposal with everything the bank or lender would need to make a decision. Do not even give them the opportunity to say, "No." Being unorganized or unprofessional will raise a red flag. Therefore, all you need to do is follow the steps in chapter 6 and you will eliminate almost every question a lender could have about you, your business, and your deal. Make sure this proposal is organized and professional looking before you move onto the next step.

Step 6:

Do you remember all of the resources I mentioned in chapter 2? These are the people and institutions you want to start sending your proposal to. All of the information and documentation is ready so now it is time to start setting up meetings and phone conferences to generate interest. You will find this to be much easier than you first thought. In preparation for this step it is helpful to begin building a lender list of potential private investors, hard money lenders, or friends and family that could potentially fund your deal. The decision for a lender to fund your deal is primarily based on the information you provide and how good your deal is. If meeting with the bank is first on your list, then try them. But if you first want to seek a private money investor, then present your deal and fill their need. Private investors want to make a return on their money because loaning money is what they do. Private investors are always in search of new deals to make money on. Your deal should be easy for you to present to them because you hold the answers to their questions in the proposal you just created. One last thing to remember is that a *"no"* is temporary. I remember early on in my career I needed to find $190,000 in 30 days or less. At this time I did not have a network of lenders as I was brand new at this. I presented my deal over and over and investors kept on saying no. But I did not quit. I kept presenting the deal until I got a yes. That was back in 2014 and that one private investor has now funded over 20 deals for us. Another interesting thing happened: a lot of the private investors that had previously said *no* to my deals came around and on the next deal said *yes*. No one wants to be the first one when you are a new real estate investor. You have to build credibility and that requires you to take action and get going. Sitting around over analyzing and overthinking will never build credibility.

Step 7:

In order to properly execute the deal with lenders, you will need to understand what is needed to secure the deal. You have all the knowledge you need to get to this point, but now I want to teach you what documents you will need to have prepared by your real estate attorney. This part of the process requires professional, legal representation.

Once you have found a lender for your deal and they have done their own underwriting, you will need to sign documents and follow certain steps to not only protect yourself but most importantly protect your investors.

The documents you will need may vary from state to state and lender to lender. The most common documents are as follows.

In no order, typical loan documents will include:

- Note/Promissory Note - spells out the terms of the loan (interest rate, term, payments, prepayment penalties, etc.)
- Deed-of-Trust or mortgage - the **mortgage** or **deed of trust** is the document that pledges the property as security for the loan.
- Purchase contract and escrow instructions - to confirm your deal and the associated deadlines you and your lender will have to meet.

- Preliminary Title Report - you and your lender should review any current liens against the property.
- Personal Guarantee - you must protect your lender.
- Documents displaying that you have the assets necessary to complete this deal and will protect your lender from a claim that this is a predatory loan.
- Use of Loan Proceeds Statement - where you declare that the use of the money and the purpose of the loan will be for a flip or rental.
- Lender Instructions - to direct escrow and title with your lender's specific instructions, including loan position, various insurance requirements, dealing with certain liens, etc.
- Lenders Title Insurance - policy with the proper endorsements.
- Fire and Liability Insurance - policy (**NOT** a homeowner's policy) this is important to protect the lender against losses. You should also include the lender's name or company as the loss payee on the policy.
- Appraisal

I could go on and on... however, I recommend you seek legal counsel to help prepare and guide you through this process. I always teach and highly recommend that any lending should be done through a properly set up corporation or legal entity such as an LLC. which stands for Limited Liability Company. I also want to point out that you should never direct the funds to your entity until after the property has properly closed and all notes and mortgages or deeds-of-trust are properly recorded and filed. Once everything is recorded, the remaining funds can then be directed to your account to begin the renovations. Proper escrowing of funds is vital. Your attorney knows the order for a real estate closing better than anyone else. First the lender agrees to loan you the funds for your property. Next the proper documents are created and signed and the lender sends the funds to the escrow account named in the note. Next the attorney or title company closes the property. Finally the note, mortgage or deed-of-trust is recorded, filed and the remaining funds are directed to your entity.

I also suggest creating a segregated bank account to keep the investors funds separate from other business expenses. Once you begin the rehab, it's important to understand that most lenders will require the rehab funds to be distributed as draws. This means you will have to do the work first and then the lender or the escrow holder will distribute the draw when the work has been completed and inspected. This may mean that you will need to advance some of the money to buy materials, pay deposits to contractors, and other required expenses. In the beginning, I used loans from my whole life policies, credit cards, and income from my job to make this happen. I always told myself, "whatever it takes"! That is exactly what I did to make my dreams a reality. I did whatever it took and whatever was necessary. You may have to do the same, and I can tell you this, <u>it will all be worth it in the long run.</u>

    The time has now come to execute your strategy. This may mean getting the house staged, cleaned, and ready to sell. Maybe it means it's time to list the property for rent so that you can begin the process of refinancing it with a bank so that the lender can be paid back and you can begin collecting passive income from the rent roll. Or it's time to leverage the property and refinance it. Maybe even apply for a home equity line of credit (HELOC) to pull the equity out and repeat the process. Eventually you can simply become the bank, which, in my opinion is the ultimate goal in this business. Now get going and repeat the process!

Chapter 8
Second Phase of Financing

It's now time to learn about the second phase. At this point you have learned all about money and how to get it. You have learned about structuring a deal and how to prepare your deals so you can present them to lenders. You also know the basics about the execution and the proper documents to use to protect your lenders and yourself. This next step will be needed when you start holding the properties and build a rental portfolio. This is how you start making money while you sleep.

When I first started buying and holding properties, I went straight to the bank for financing. This was a difficult learning lesson since the bank typically funds 75-80% of the purchase price. If you only do a few deals, this will not be a problem. However, I did not want to do a few—I wanted to do far more than a few and this is where I had to learn this strategy. If you want to scale your business, your income, and your net worth, you will have to continue buying additional rental properties. If you use traditional bank financing, you will have to pay 20-25% plus closing costs out of pocket. You will also have to pay for the renovation costs too. You do not have to be good at math to figure out that you will eventually go broke. This is why I had to change the way I bought rentals. I use the BRRRR strategy (since I live in Buffalo, New York where it can get quite cold, I renamed it, "The Buffalo BRRRR"). This requires us to buy properties that are significantly undervalued then renovate the property to force appreciation back into the property. If you follow the formula you should have adequate equity in the property to cover at least 20%. The property may have more equity than the bank-required 20-25% after you are done with the renovations. This means you may be able to take some cash out when you refinance. This type of refinance is actually called a "cash out refi." The other thing you need to understand is this: most banks will lend

75-80% of the appraised value on a refinance. This is far better than getting 75-80% financing on the purchase price only. From my experience, most community banks are lending on renovated and tenant occupied properties. I have successfully done this over and over again and we have students doing this on a regular basis. In full transparency it is important to remember that for this to work you have to qualify for bank financing. That means you need good credit scores, debt-to-income that is within the banks guidelines, and of course reportable income to show you can support the payments. Also, I want to bring to your attention that some banks require seasoning. That means that you will have to hold the property for a certain time frame before the bank will allow you to refinance. In this situation I would suggest looking for banks that do not require seasoning. If that does not work just make sure the rental income covers your private lenders interest payments and the other carry costs. I start the refinance process before the project is done; I get the ball rolling to save on time. Time is money and I want to get a jump on this when the renovation is almost finished. Sometimes I have to put off the appraiser for a week or two but at least the paperwork has been submitted at that point.

By using this strategy we have been able to build a sizable rental portfolio comprised of completely renovated, rent-positive properties. The best part of this is that we have been able to do this with very little money out of pocket. The thing I focus on is the cash-on-cash return; I want to maximize the return on the money I have invested. I never exceed 80% of the current property value. At any given time I know I have 20% equity in my properties. It's a safety buffer if things were to ever go down in value. The other thing I love about this is that you are building a portfolio by acquiring properties for under current market value. I see so many investors overpaying for properties, especially rentals. I wish I could tell everyone how to find lucrative off-market deals. Then again, that would give away all the secrets and I like to reserve those for people like you who are part of our network and the real estate community we are building. By now you should be getting a good idea of how money works in real estate and how you can use and leverage assets to build your empire.

Chapter 9
Get to Your Goal Faster

One of the golden rules in life is, "if you give, you get." I live my life by this and it has proven to be true over and over. However, the "get" part does not reward you immediately —you can't just give once and expect the universe to reward you. You have to always give unconditionally no matter what. I have believed in this concept all of my life and it has served me very well. This booklet is just another piece of my give back.

After my snowboard career ended with a bad injury, I went into depression when I couldn't bounce back and be at the top. I trained harder, practiced longer, but no matter how hard I tried, I could not beat the new generation of fearless athletes. I almost wanted to quit all together. The fire inside me was running out of fuel. Then something strange happened: I got a call from a friend asking me if I would coach and train a snowboard team whose team members needed an extra push. I said no at first because I initially thought, *I'm above this... I am a pro-snowboarder; why would I coach a team?... I don't have time for this...and the money is not very good, and I could make much more just working instead of coaching kids...* I don't have any children so I don't yet understand what being a parent is all about I don't know the feeling you get from being a parent and why parents decide to coach little league or help at Brownies. I have never been a fan of kids—primarily because I was never around them. I came up with every excuse as to why this was not the opportunity for me. Then, after weeks of thinking about it and trying to rationalize with myself, I finally decided to try it out. This ended up completely changing the course of my life and it resurrected the joy I had lost when I felt snowboarding was over for me.

The first year I helped take that team to multiple podium wins at national competitions and at that moment, I experienced the same feeling

I used to get when I won and stood on that podium. The only difference was this time the sense of accomplishment and joy was even greater. I helped these kids achieve a monumental victory in their lives; the same victory I once accomplished, but this time the feeling was even better! I went on to be the head coach for this amazing team for 6 years. The pay was not great, and some days it was so cold I could barely breathe, and some days I just did not want to be there... but the second those kids started showing up ready to live their dreams, I snapped into my old mindset and I too was ready to relive my dreams with them.

Years later my wife and I founded Flipout Academy. We wanted to create a results-based real estate education platform focusing solely on the results of our students. We wanted to bring students through a systematized process of learning followed by application of knowledge to get results just like I did in snowboarding. The results our student are getting is life-changing. They are learning how to chase their dreams just like I used to with snowboarding and just like Lorissa and I did when we started in the real estate business. We wanted to create a trade school for real estate investors. I can certainly say our journey has just begun. I want to teach as many people as humanly possible how money works in real estate. We created a curriculum called Money School to achieve that goal. We very recently began teaching kids ages 7-17 how to be money smart; their curriculum is titled Money School: Money's Cool.

Now that we are all thinking about giving, I wanted to use this chapter to talk about what you have just gained. Not only will this information impact your life, it will help the people in your circle. Your private lenders, your friends, your family, and your acquaintances can all be positively influenced if you let them in on what you know. The returns and interest you pay the lenders allow them to earn a more consistent income, live better lives, enjoy a better retirement... and the best part is it's all secured by real estate! Having been a financial advisor, I can tell you first hand that if my clients could have earned 8-12% interest on their investments, they could have done things differently. People could retire earlier and with more confidence. Parents could accumulate more savings to pay for college and higher education. I could go on and on with this, but I am sure you get the big picture here. Real estate holds the answer to so many problems we face in life. The sad thing is that most people will never know it was within their grasps the whole time. If people simply knew how money worked in real estate, people would be able to live better lives. I am certainly not saying it's the answer to everything, but I am saying it's a small step in the right direction and a great way for lenders and investors to diversify their investments and stabilize there returns. We live in a world that revolves around cash flow. Everything we have discussed has involved cash flow and money. Now it is your duty to go out there and tell as many people you know about this. When you have a great deal and you are hesitant to ask friends and family to fund your deal, you should change your mindset and think differently. Think about what's in it for them...higher interest rates, consistent monthly payments, security, a tangible asset backing the loan and note...etc. Whether you know it or not, these things are not found in most investment opportunities out there. This is rare and this is amazing! So be bold, be fearless, and apply the information I've presented in this booklet so that you can create the life you dream about!

The Private Money Guide: Real Estate Edition

Chapter 10
Strategies to Cashing Out

Once you start building your portfolio of properties, a lot of things will begin to change. Obviously, your income will increase, the value of your properties increase and new opportunities will start to present themself to you. After the first few successful deals, you will have built up valuable credibility. The first few lenders will have been paid back and they will likely be eager to do additional deals with you. They will also begin to tell others about their experience and then other people will begin to ask if you have any deals that need funding. Your peers and fellow real estate investors will begin to recognize that you are doing well and that you have funding available which will result in them bringing more deals to you. The entire system you created will start to get easier and easier. The one thing you can't forget is that you must continue to stay active, attend networking events, REIAs, and other related functions. You cannot ever forget to be persistent and consistent. This is one of the most important things to your continued success.

You will begin to work smarter instead of harder, which will allow you to start working on higher-level real estate deals and those real estate deals will once again require additional funding. At this point, you can start leveraging the portfolio you have created. Properties that you bought a few years earlier will have appreciated and that equity can be tapped into just like you learned in earlier chapters of this booklet. Banks will be willing to give you working lines of credit based on your assets and the additional income the portfolio generates. This is the natural cycle of this business. Once you start to leverage your equity, you will have access to less expensive money. Money that can be used for different types of projects that you may not have had access to earlier on. One of the smartest things we have done is to loan our money out to other investors. Becoming the bank, in my opinion, is the ultimate goal. You have all the knowledge on how to underwrite the deals, how to protect yourself, and how to secure your loans, you know how to manage a real estate project and you have all the experience that you will need to see the entire process through. **The best way to learn is to do**, you have done exactly that so now it is time to shift into high gear. Some of you will continue to do flips and build your rental portfolios, some of you will use your resources to become the bank and some of you will go on to be developers. There is no right or wrong path. There is only your chosen path.

About 8 years ago, I had an idea to take on a townhouse development in an amazing ski town called Ellicottville. This project included buying vacant land, re-surveying the land into 9 parcels which would hold two townhouses each, installing the infrastructure needed to do the development, and then develop three-phases of townhouses. This was a big project for me so I asked a few investors I had met if they would like to be part of this opportunity. They all happily agreed. The biggest hurdle in this project was the large sum of money we needed in order to pay for all of the early construction expenses. In a project like this, it is not easy to get bank funding for the initial soft costs. This is where leverage was my best friend. I had several properties that had appreciated significantly over the years. I began the refinance process on these properties and that provided the necessary funding to get phase 1 off the ground. With a lot of help from my partners, we were able to complete and sell out the first phase and today we are well on our way to completing phase 2. Once we got the first unit built we took the deal to a local community bank and they gave us a sizeable construction loan that has been the main funding source for the project ever since. This project was one that would have never been possible if I did not learn and follow the exact things I have been talking about in this booklet. This townhouse project is one of many projects we have done over the years. I certainly can say that my wife and I have more money available to us than we can find deals for. On a weekly basis we have investors asking if we have any deals they can fund or joint venture in. I am not saying this to brag, I simply want you to understand what the possibilities are. Just to put things into perspective, my wife and I started going full force into real estate five short years ago in 2014. It did not take us decades to build up to this level and if you work hard and hustle you can do the same.

As I mentioned earlier, I did not come from money— I grew up in a lower middle-class family with only enough money to make ends meet. I have struggled, I have almost gone bankrupt, I have had to sell things just to get to the next month, but there is never a moment when I regret any of it. Today we have a rental portfolio that generates just under a million dollars in gross revenue, we have a wholesale business that generates a six figure income, we still flip houses and most importantly, we love our lifestyle. This is all because of the principles in this booklet. If you can get good at money, the rest will fall into place. If you don't get good at money, the rest will happen but it will be a struggle. I have seen so many so-called "real estate gurus" show off their flashy lifestyles: cars, houses, trips, and they make it all look so easy. If you look deeper into their lives, most of them are all smoke and mirrors. I always suggest reading the book, "The Millionaire Next Door" by Thomas J. Stanley. You will get a better grasp of who has the money. Then you should take notes and realize that those are the people you should start talking to about your deals. Don't buy into the hype you see on social media... this business is not easy, but this business will change your life, that much I can promise. Start with the money because that is the source. It always has been and it always will be.

If you implement these steps in this booklet and you do it consistently and persistently I can promise you a few things will happen:

- You will find people to talk to about funding your deals
- You will be able to achieve far more than you ever imagined possible because you will understand how money works
- This will impact your life

I am certain many people will apply this knowledge and they will get results. I also realize many people will pick up this booklet, do nothing, and continue to wonder why money is so hard to find.

"Opportunity is missed by most people because it is dressed in overalls and looks like work." - Thomas Edison

Please keep this booklet close by, tell people about it, or give your copy away to someone. Remember, if you give... you get. When you raise your first million by using the strategies and principles I have taught you, contact me and let's chat about what's next.

Chapter 10: Strategies to Cashing Out

These are your next steps with Flipout Academy and Money School. Don't kick the can down the road any longer! Do it now!

SIGN UP TODAY:

Money School's Inner Circle Mastermind Event
www.moneyschoolrei.com/innercircle
Mastering Wholesaling Webinar
www.flipouttraining.com.

If you are interested in our Money School Mastermind group or one-to-one coaching programs send an email to support@flipoutacademy.com

If you would like to set up a Self-Directed IRA this is who we use
Sign up to open your Self Directed IRA account
https://www.horizontrust.com/flipout/

If you would like to inquire about our group discount pricing if you are buying books for your event please go to this link: moneyschoolrei.com/book

Recommended Books:
Never Split the Difference by Chris Voss
What Would the Rockefellers Do by Garrett Gunderson
The Obstacle is the Way by Ryan Holiday
Think and Grow Rich by Napoleon Hill
Three Feet from Gold by Greg S. Reid & Sharon L. Lechter
Steve Jobs by Walter Isaacson
The Warren Buffett Way by Robert B. Hagstrom
The Intelligent Investor by Benjamin Graham
Sell or be Sold by Grant Cardone
Be Obsessed or Be Average by Grant Cardone
Get Out of Your Own Way by Bob McIntosh

Made in the USA
Lexington, KY
25 October 2019